Advance praise for 'Renting Dirt'

Until I read *Renting Dirt*, I didn't think much about own-ing an RV park. I pretty much took it for granted that it was a fairly straightforward process—buy or build the park, maintain it, price a campsite fairly, and promote it. The customers will come. But no, it's a whole lot more than that.

Nobody in the campground industry, to my knowledge, has ever written as candidly about how much work is involved in operating an RV park. If they have, I've never seen it. Andy's book is an eye-opener. Anyone thinking of building or buying an RV park should absolutely read this book before they get very far into the process. I believe some would-be buyers think that operating such a business is a way to earn a good living in the outdoors, maybe experience nature, meet nice people and be their own boss. Yes, that's part of it.

But, as I have learned from *Renting Dirt*, it can be very difficult and, at times, exhausting work, physically, mentally and emotionally. And as Andy points out, pleasing campers can be maddening—even impossible, at times. My fellow RVers should read this book; they'll have a whole new appreciation for the own-ers and operators of the parks where they stay.

I would never think a book on this subject could be a page-turner, but it is. I had a hard time putting it down.

—*Chuck Woodbury,*
Publisher, RVtravel.com

Dedicated to my wife, Carin, without whom none of this would have happened; and to both of our dads, because Carin thinks they would have gotten a kick out of it all.

Abundant thanks also to my diligent proofreaders, sounding boards and critics: Ron and Sandra Chen, Ann Zipser and Joanna Elm. Any surviving errors or grammatical embarrassments are, needless to say, entirely the author's fault.

Renting Dirt

An unfertilized (no BS) look at what it takes to run a campground and RV park

Andy Zipser

Photographs by Andy Zipser
Photograph p.21 courtesy of Gene Hayden

Mint Spring Publishing
P.O. Box 114
Mint Spring, VA 24463

All other communications may be directed to:
azipser@renting-dirt.com

ISBN: 978-1-7377750-0-3 (Paperback)
ISBN: 978-1-7377750-1-0 (eBook)

Library of Congress Control Number: 2021916781

Printed in the United States of America, 2021.

Contents

Glossary   6

Introduction   9

CHAPTER 1
Oh captain, my captain   13

CHAPTER 2
A little slice of heaven   21

CHAPTER 3
Sometimes, it is skin deep   31

CHAPTER 4
The customer is not always right   45

CHAPTER 5
A walk on the dark side   59

CHAPTER 6
One big, happy family   71

CHAPTER 7
Spitting out the yellow Kool Aid   83

CHAPTER 8
It takes a village   91

CHAPTER 9
The Disney-fication of camping   101

CHAPTER 10
Whip-sawed by the pandemic   111

CHAPTER 11
Throwing in the towel   121

Afterword   125

Glossary

NON-CAMPERS MAY BE UNFAMILIAR with some of the terms and acronyms in this book, so here's a short reference guide. The RVers in the crowd can readily skip this section.

ARVC: the awkward acronym for the National Association of RV Parks and Campgrounds, the only U.S. and Canadian trade group representing campground owners and operators.

ATV: All-Terrain Vehicle, usually a four-wheeled off-road vehicle that, paradoxically, does not have a crash protection system and partly for that reason is not street-legal.

FAQ: Frequently Asked Questions.

GIS: Government Information System mapping, an invaluable online resource for anyone wanting to understand land ownership and uses.

RV: short for "recreational vehicle," which can include both towables (fifth-wheels, travel trailers and pop-ups) and driveables (classes A, B and C, plus pick-up campers and roof-top carriers).

- **Fifth-wheel:** a trailer with a goose-neck hitch that fits into the bed of a pick-up truck.
- **Travel trailer:** a more conventional trailer, with a hitch that fits onto the ball of a receiving hitch mounted to a tow vehicle.
- **Pop-up:** a travel trailer with canvas sides whose roof

can be raised when camping and lowered when traveling, creating a low profile.

- **Class A:** motor coaches, resembling large buses.
- **Class B:** converted vans, ranging in size from a regular cargo van to 24-foot "touring coaches" with extended ceilings.
- **Class C:** midway between class A and class B motorhomes, these are RVs built on a cutaway chassis that allows access from the cab and are readily recognizable by the over-the-cab protrusion of the living space.
- **Pick-up Camper:** a camper that slides into the bed of a pick-up truck, with an over-the-cab extension similar to those on class C's.

Boondocking: RV camping, usually on public land, without utility hook-ups.

Franchise: a right or license granted by a company (in this context either Jellystone or KOA) to a business to use its logo, trademark and brand name in exchange for up-front franchise fees and a percentage of the business's income.

Full-timers: RVers who live year-round in their RVs, and who may or may not still own a "sticks-and-bricks" house that they use as a home base.

Seasonal sites: RV sites that are reserved for a month (or more) at a time, sometimes as summer vacation homes, sometimes for short-term housing by students, itinerant workers, traveling nurses and other nomads.

Single-wide and **double-wide:** house trailers manufactured off-site and towed to their location in 12-foot wide sections, two sections pieced together comprising a double-wide.

Slide-outs: sometimes finicky RV room extenders that slide out on rails, incorporated into just about every RV manufactured these days other than pop-ups, Class Bs and Airstream trailers.

Snowbirds: RVers—often full-timers—who travel with the seasons, heading north in the summers to escape the heat and south in the winter to get away from the snow.

Introduction

IN THE PAST DECADE, the allure of hopping into a home on wheels and taking it just about anywhere has exploded worldwide, but especially here in the United States. A pastime once associated with retired old white people has blossomed across all ages and income levels, attracting new interest from non-white couples and families as well. Millennials and GenX-ers who can work remotely have discovered that there is an alternative to being stuck in a cramped or expensive apartment—as long as they can get a good wi-fi connection. And as if all that weren't enough, the Covid-19 pandemic opened a lot of people's eyes to the travel and vacation possibilities of a lifestyle that allows virtually total social distancing, complete with private bathroom, kitchen, bedroom, and an unparalleled ventilation system known as the Great Outdoors.

All those campers and their RVs (not to mention the hordes who don't want or can't afford an RV, but who want to go tent camping or to rent a cabin) have to go *somewhere*. For some, that means heading into the backcountry, on foot or in a four-wheeler, tenting or boondocking on land overseen by the Bureau of Land Management. For others it means ferreting out a site in a federal or state park or forest, where there's room for privacy but amenities (such as decent wi-fi or a sewer connection) are severely limited.

And some significant percentage, with deeper pockets or less taste for adventure or a bigger desire for creature comforts, will look for accommodations at a commercial campground.

This book is a personal look at that last option: commercial campgrounds as a business and what it takes to run them, as well as their customers and what they expect and demand.

Back in 2011, when my wife and I first started looking into buying an RV park, the campground business was just emerging from the battering it had absorbed in the Great Recession. Mom-and-pop campgrounds were a sleepy backwater in the hospitality industry, a relatively cheap way to have a vacation in the great outdoors. They still can be—I don't mean to overstate the case—but in recent years, demand has grown so much that it sometimes outstrips supply, putting upward pressure on prices. That, in turn, has attracted growing interest from investors seeking the next big thing, with all but the smallest campgrounds getting targeted by monied interests—who, in turn, push prices even higher.

This outpouring of camping interest, ginned up by ever more pervasive marketing images of smiling families gathered around a campfire, toasting marshmallows and hot dogs, is crowding facilities, stressing staffs and overwhelming the environment that's ostensibly being celebrated. Meanwhile, the Great Outdoors ain't what it used to be, either, thanks to accelerating climate change and extreme weather on one hand, and the relentless Disney-fication of campgrounds themselves on the other.

One can't be immersed in this world without being affected by these developments. Some campground owners, and we know quite a few, have grown bitter and cynical over the years. At the other end of the spectrum are those—often long-timers, whose lives are fully invested in their properties—who deny the changes going on around them and retreat into a strained optimism. My wife and I are much closer to the former, but like to think we escaped before we sank too deep into the morass. The reader can decide whether we succeeded.

This book, then, is also a description of our transformation, from wide-eyed entrepreneurs risking their life's savings to the somewhat jaundiced veterans of a demanding consumer culture that we are today. We learned a lot along the way, about ourselves as much as about the world we live in. Others who might be contemplating a similar journey—as many RVers have wistfully shared with us—may find our experiences instructive, either as a user's manual or as a cautionary note. And those who merely wish to enjoy a campground without owning one may at least understand why there's more to this business than merely "renting a piece of dirt," as some have dismissively summarized it.

—September, 2021

Setting sail on the Walnut Hills playground.

1. O captain, my captain

THE POUNDING CAME after 10 p.m., when I was already in my pajamas and about to go to bed. It was January and cold outside, and my immediate response was one of irritation. "Who the hell could that be?" I asked my wife as I strode to the door and pulled it open.

Standing outside the storm door, bundled up against the drifting snow, was someone I couldn't recognize holding up a fragmentary piece of metal that reflected the porch light. "I'm sorry to bother you," he started, voice muffled by the scarf wrapped around his head, "but I've never had this happen to me before." I peered closer. What he was holding looked like half of a door key.

"Me neither," I replied, opening the storm door to let him in. "Me neither."

*   *   *

Eighteen months earlier, sitting in a motel conference room in Tennessee with a couple of dozen other prospective campground owners, the last thing on my mind was the possibility that for almost a decade my life would cease to be my own. My wife, Carin, and I were attending a two-day seminar hosted by Darrell Hess, a real estate broker who specializes in campgrounds and RV parks. His job was to educate us on the complexities of buying a campground, and ideally also to move some of his own inventory. Ours was to learn as much as we could about an industry and a lifestyle that we'd experienced only as consumers—as "campers," although we'd eventually learn that the label is too amorphous to be meaningful.

But even that experience was limited. Years earlier, when our younger daughter was in her early teens, we'd borrowed a class C motorhome from Carin's dad, and later another from a friend, to tour the Midwest and up into Canada. We'd gone as far west as Devil's Tower and as far east as the Bay of Fundy, explored the Wisconsin Dells and stumbled across the House on the Rock, followed the Laura Ingalls Wilder trail and watched the live outdoor presentation of her life held every July in Walnut Grove, Minnesota. Little did we anticipate the connection that would run from Walnut Grove to Walnut Hills, Virginia, some 20 years later.

And as we traveled, we did what so many RVing couples do: we'd sit around a campfire, wine glasses in hand, and listen to the crickets and tree frogs. We'd look at the night sky, and the fireflies winking at us from the surrounding woods. We'd breathe in the crisp air and relax into the evening and then say to each other, somewhat wistfully, "Wouldn't it be neat to actually own a place like this?"

Oh, those crazy kids.

The years passed, and then a couple of decades. We eventually bought a small pop-up, and then graduated to a small travel trailer and went on more limited excursions, to the Outer Banks or to the Smokies. But my job as editor of a union publication didn't give me the kind of time off required for more far-flung adventures, and in any case, Carin was growing ever less keen on long road trips. The memory of those lazy fireside musings grew faint, then disappeared from consciousness altogether—for me. Not so for Carin.

One evening, in late 2011, I announced that I had decided to retire. Not right away, not for several months, but soon. I was about to become fully vested in my defined benefit pension plan, and at 64 I'd be old enough to start claiming early Social Security benefits, so we'd have enough to live on. I had grown weary of the commute from our home in the northern Virginia suburb of Manassas to downtown Washington, D.C. And truth be told, my employer at the Newspaper Guild— tiring of my constant resistance to making our union's in-house newspaper a propaganda sheet—was eager to show me the door, anyway. It looked like a win-win to me.

Carin had other thoughts. "What are you going to do with yourself?" she asked.

"What do you mean?" I replied.

"Well, how are you going to spend your days? What will you be doing once you don't have to go to an office every day?"

"Oh," I replied airily, "there are lots of things I could get into. Maybe I'll try a little freelancing. And now that I've set up a woodworking shop in the garage, I thought I'd try my hand at making furniture—perhaps doll furniture, to go with the doll clothes you've been sewing. There are bicycle trips I could take. And don't forget my work as an EMT and volunteer firefighter— that requires constant training. I don't think I'll have any trouble staying busy."

That's what I said, but mostly what Carin heard was "bicycle trips." In her mind that signaled an unending procession of ever longer absences, bicycle trips to be augmented by backpacking excursions, both of which would take me progressively ever farther afield. Our small travel trailer, once a means of mutual escape from the pressures and tedium of daily life, would become my magic carpet out of our house—and therefore out of her homebound existence. Carin was about to become a wanderer's widow and she didn't like it one bit, and so an alternative had to be found.

Which, a few days later, she advanced over dinner. "Do you remember," she asked, gazing over the top of her glass of Beaujolais in a presumably unconscious reprise of that decades-old musing, "how we used to sit around a campfire and tell each other how neat it would be to own a place like that? Well, how about . . . ."

And so here we were, with just that slender a foundation on which to build a future, listening to Darrell Hess extol the many attractions of owning a campground as he demystified the ins-and-outs of campground pricing and financing. Owning a campground means owning your own future, he explained—you make your own hours and answer to no one but yourself, and you get out of it what you put in. How many jobs can you find in which you directly reap the rewards of your efforts, in which every day is unlike the one before it or the one after, in which you can build a legacy for your kids and grandkids?

But buying and selling a campground is a fraught business, Darrell added, mostly because no one knows what they're doing. The biggest purchase most people have ever made was to buy a home, which in most cases meant working in an established marketplace. But with campgrounds? Most campground owners have never sold a campground. Most campground buyers have never bought a campground. Most bankers have never had a campground in their portfolios and have no idea how to assess the risk of financing one, and most bank appraisers have never appraised a campground and have little clue as to how it should be valued.

Talk about the blind leading the blind!

Fortunately, Darrell had a formula. Even better, Darrell was (and is) a licensed broker who could help us, the potential buyers, properly evaluate a property so we wouldn't lose our shirts—even as he educated sellers on how to value their campgrounds, a role I didn't properly appreciate until much later, when we repeatedly encountered buyers with over-the-moon price expectations. (Meanwhile, the inherent conflict of interest in having a broker represent both sides of a transaction never occurred to us, but we were fortunate that our first deep dive into the business was with an honest one; some others we encountered later were not as scrupulous.)

What are you paying for when you buy a campground? Darrell would ask rhetorically. Is it the land? The improvements? The existing customer base? Room for expansion? Lack of competition?

All those things are not unimportant, especially as you evaluate a property's future potential—but what you're paying for is cash flow. And for reasons too esoteric to expand on here, having to do with capitalization rates and investment risk, Darrell's formula generally required a campground's selling price to fall within a range of three to four times annual gross revenue. Did the campground pull in $200,000 last year? Then it shouldn't cost more than $600,000 to $800,000 this year, and at that level of revenue, probably closer to the low end. Is a campground listed for $3 million? It'd better have at least $750,000 on the books for last year.

That rule of thumb became a cardinal principle for us in the months ahead. But at that moment, sitting in a motel conference room and nodding our heads in agreement with Darrell's expanding line of financial logic, it belatedly struck me that we were talking about really serious money. When we bought our house in Manassas, more than a decade earlier, Carin got sweaty palms over a purchase price of $165,000. Now we were contemplating spending multiples of that for a business that we did not understand, with no idea of how we were going to raise the 25% down-payment that was the bare minimum required, and even less idea of how we were going to finance the rest.

And for what? Because as it soon also became obvious, living year-round on a campground is very different from camping in one for a few days or a week, and very, very different from living in a three-bedroom home in suburbia with sheet-rocked walls and a foundation. As Darrell flipped through case study after study of sales he had brokered, it was clear that very few campgrounds provided substantial living quarters for owners or managers. Most offered single- or double-wide trailers; some actually relied on fifth-wheels for housing. Lacking adequate insulation and often marked by shoddy construction, house trailers are cold in winter, hot in summer and dusty just about all the time if the campground has gravel roads, as many do.

But not to worry! As Darrell also explained, buying a campground also means buying a lifestyle—and that lifestyle is not one of brick homes with white picket fences. It means walking to work instead of commuting, of working outdoors instead of in a stuffy office building, of having ready access to amenities that only a sliver of the general population can afford, like a swimming pool and weekend concerts and fishing in your own lake. It means relating to people who are out to have a good time rather than stressed out co-workers and urban dwellers.

In other words, in addition to being in control of your own life instead of having it controlled by others, owning a campground means living a life that others can only envy. Campground ownership, when you got right down to it, is the American dream distilled to its very essence. *Viva la vida!*

*   *   *

I gestured to our visitor to sit in our living room, then asked him to explain what was going on. Unwrapping his head scarf, he once again held up the partial key as he said, "I don't know what happened. I put the key in the lock and turned it, and it just snapped off."

"You can't get in?" I asked, still unwilling to believe what I was seeing.

"No, we can't. The lock is jammed. We got in earlier with no trouble, but after we unloaded the car we went out to dinner—and then this happened," he said. "My girlfriend is out in the car right now, but we're cold and tired and can't get our things, and we have no place to go. I don't know what to do."

"That's okay—that's what we're here for," I said, as cheerily as I could muster. "We'll get you some bedding and put you in another cabin for the night, then figure out in the morning how we're going to get your stuff. We may have to drill out the lock, and it's too late for that right now, but don't worry— it'll all work out!"

And on that upbeat note I went to get dressed, then out into the snow-blown night to secure linens and a new key, walking to work in the dark. Captain of my fate, master of all I surveyed.

Feeding the ducks.

2. A little slice of heaven

DARRELL HESS'S SEMINAR was only the first step in our self-education program, as Carin and I subsequently sought out the relatively few books written on campground acquisition, scoured the internet for advice and signed up as associate members of ARVC, an industry trade group. But we also discovered that we had a lot to learn about our own expectations—that once we started putting flesh on a bare-bones idea, each of us could end up with remarkably different ideas from the other, or from what we had hazily contemplated a couple of decades earlier.

The first big question was: where? Where did we want to create our little paradise? If we were going to move, how much difference could there be between a move of 300 miles and 3,000? And if the difference wasn't all that great, why not think about relocating to the lush rain forests of the Pacific northwest? Or the clean, arid sweep of the desert southwest? What of the mountain vistas of the Rockies? All seemed alluring—to me.

Not so for Carin, who despite her past camping experiences harbors a deep distrust of Mother Nature. Where I was exhilarated by wilderness and extreme landscapes, she saw menace and danger. I had spent months over my lifetime backpacking in the High Sierra, the Grand Canyon, Yellowstone, Mount Rainier and sections of the Appalachian Trail; Carin's idea of "roughing it," as she told me from the very beginning of our relationship, was a motel with a black and white TV. For her—and therefore for both of us—the thought of uprooting our lives and moving to an area where we might be buffeted by forces beyond our control was a non-starter, no matter how many fringe benefits might come with the location.

So. No earthquakes (goodbye, West Coast!). No hurricanes (so long, Gulf Coast!). Most critically—for someone who grew up in western Illinois—absolutely no tornadoes (farewell to the Midwest!).

By chance, we discovered an on-line map that plotted exactly those variables. And while any of the unholy trinity can conceivably occur almost anywhere, the map showed only two areas in the lower 48 that are relatively earthquake-, tornado- and hurricane-free: the Four-Corners region of the American southwest, and an area of the upper Appalachians extending into parts of Virginia, Ohio, New York, and Pennsylvania. Our search now had a focus.

Initially, we let our fingers do the walking, exploring literally scores of campgrounds listed for sale on various websites and by half-a-dozen or so brokers specializing in recreational properties. We quickly learned to screen prospects through a handful of criteria: where is it located? how many acres? how many sites? how many *improved* sites? how many seasonal campers? how long a season? what kind of owner housing? And, always, how much do they want?

When we started, we didn't know just what kind of campground we were seeking, but as we researched the market some basic requirements came into focus. We didn't want a mere seven or 10 or even 15 acres, as described in many of the listings, even though they claimed to have 50 or 80 or 100 sites. A campground, we agreed, needed to have elbow room, and jamming seven or 10 RV sites to an acre (and in some cases more!) sounded claustrophobic at best and like a trailer park slum at worst.

We also decided we didn't want too many seasonal or long-term campers—that our emphasis would be on transient campers looking for an overnight stop, or those out for a few days or a week for some back-to-nature rest and relaxation. We wanted to own a recreational facility, not a residential one, and we recoiled at the thought of having a critical mass of people staying month after month, gradually over-running their sites and over-stepping other boundaries. Meeting numerous campground owners at ARVC seminars, I'd heard too many stories of inmates taking over the asylum—of seasonal or more permanent campers who'd start taking ownership of a property, and not usually in a good way.

And as we began looking along the east coast as far north as upstate New York, Vermont and Maine, we eventually began to edge away from the idea of extreme winter weather. Both of us had grown up in four-season country, and we liked the idea of fall foliage and brisk winter days that would decimate bothersome insect populations. But "the lake effect" was no joke, we learned, as we reluctantly wrote off a couple of possibilities outside Buffalo and Rochester. Upper New England was no better—not with annual snowfalls upwards of 80 inches. And while many campground owners in those areas close shop in October or November and head south for four or five months, we concluded we'd rather operate a four-season campground, even if at a slower pace for part of the year. The bills would be rolling in year-round, after all, even if the receipts weren't.

We also soon wrote off the entire Four-Corners area, as yet another environmental threat became too obvious to ignore. Although we were both familiar with the desert, having lived in Phoenix for more than a decade in the 'Seventies and 'Eighties, it quickly became apparent that something more extreme had started happening. As we looked at rainfall records, familiarized ourselves with the over-pumping of the region's aquifers and read news reports of the extreme drought that was shaping up, we realized that a campground without a reliable water supply had at best a tenuous future. Campers can always pack up and go elsewhere; campgrounds can't.

We therefore scratched New Mexico, Arizona and Utah off our list, and just like that, what had started as a wide-ranging contemplation of the entire lower 48 states had narrowed to the Appalachian region—yet even much of that reduced target area soon proved problematic.

One of our most promising early prospects was in central western Pennsylvania, a state with a surprisingly large RVing population. This particular campground had it all, including heavily wooded grounds, a well-stocked roadside store, lots of area tourism and a half-dozen beautiful split-log dwellings. It also happened to sit above the Marcellus formation, a broad swath of gas-infused shale that sweeps in a southwest curve from Syracuse, New York to the southern end of West Virginia, underlying all of that state plus most of western Pennsylvania and New York, as well as eastern Ohio.

Right across the road from the campground was a separate parcel, a 500-acre gas field that the owner had been selling off in one-acre lots for summer homes and cabins, including four of the campground's beautiful split-log dwellings that I'd been admiring. Unfortunately, the gas field owner had gone bankrupt and then died, and in the legal limbo that followed, no one was maintaining four dozen or so gas wells scattered about the property—gas wells that periodically and unpredictably would burst into flame. When asked about such flare-ups, the campground owner shrugged and said he and his son or other neighbors would "take care" of such eruptions, as if they were no more troublesome than putting out the garbage. I wasn't as sanguine.

Boning up on the still relatively new industrial practice of fracking after I returned home, Carin and I concluded that using the earth for recreation was simply not compatible with using it for resource extraction. Who would want to camp near a site that might explode in flame at any time? And what of the gas field's long-term impact on our groundwater supplies? As we learned more about these and other fracking complications, including mini-quakes and land subsidence, we reluctantly decided to cross off our list any campground in an oil shale region.

Meanwhile, as our horizons kept shrinking, our requirements for what we needed were growing, as first one and then the second of our married daughters expressed an interest in joining our venture. And although each couple agreed that at least one of its members would work full-time at the campground, contributing their sweat equity to its financial success, neither had any money to chip in for the initial purchase. That meant we had to find a property that would generate enough income to sustain three families, rather than just one, as well as provide sufficient housing for everyone. A purchase we had once thought we could make comfortably was now going to strain our resources, as we went from looking at campgrounds priced at around $500,000 to campgrounds more than triple that amount.

As we learned more about our own needs and expectations, we also started learning more about the needs and expectations of the people we would face on the other side of any transaction—mainly the campground owners, and to some extent the brokers representing them. One of the most surprising revelations was how many owners clearly were ambivalent about walking away from a home and business that had consumed a significant part of their lives. Sometimes this bubbled up in downright hostility, as with the Ohio woman who ostensibly was trying to sell her campground but who greeted me with a scowl, ignored my outstretched hand and barked, "So before we even start, can you tell me if I'm wasting my time talking to you?"

At other times, that ambivalence exploded into view only as we drew closer to a deal, sinking any possible sale. In one case early in our search, as we seriously contemplated making an offer on a campground in Vermont, the owner nervously asked about our plans for two small homes on the property, which were then occupied by tenants. When we reminded her that we had stated at the outset that we were looking for adequate housing for three couples, it was as though a wall had slammed down between us and what had been a cordial relationship suddenly became frosty.

In another instance, we had already prepared a written contract offer for a campground near Boone, North Carolina, when the owner suddenly started back-peddling, asking in effect if we would be willing to accept her as a silent partner. When we eventually understood what she meant—that we would operate the campground, but she would have veto power over any decisions we made in the first five years—we headed for the exit.

Many campground owners, we also learned, had exaggerated ideas of what their properties were worth. Take, for example, a 13-acre riverside campground that we looked at before our daughters jumped into the game. Although with less acreage than we preferred, at 54 RV sites it wasn't too crowded and, indeed, was small enough for Carin and me to manage with only minimal additional staff. And its canoe and kayak livery, plus a store with a beer and wine license, held the promise of additional revenue streams that could provide us with a decent income. Still, as with any property, there were drawbacks.

Judging by its photographs, the place looked a bit shabby. Access was via narrow, winding country roads far from any major traffic artery. And, like most riverside campgrounds, this property clearly had contended with flooding in past years. The biggest red flag, however, was the owner's reluctance to provide any revenue numbers, making us wonder if it was generating enough business to justify its $1.3 million price tag. When the owner kept ducking the issue, I finally asked her bluntly how she'd come up with her sales price.

Simple, she replied—appraised values for riverfront acreage in her county ranged from $48,000 to $80,000 an acre. When

I pointed out that her asking price was even higher, at $100,000 an acre, she had a ready if inapt response. "Our property was platted as a residential development, and certainly that would be considered the highest and best use," she responded in an email exchange. "We have a beautiful piece of property, and it wouldn't make sense to give it away just because the income of the business does not justify the cost." I thought that was a shockingly frank admission and told her we weren't looking to build a subdivision.

But that would-be seller's reasoning, while self-defeating, was typical of the kind of mental trap we repeatedly encountered: campground owners who were too invested in an idea of what their property was worth to step back and look at it from a prospective buyer's point of view. Often, they already knew they were expecting too much, but they just couldn't help themselves—just as was true of this woman, even after her campground had been on the market for several years without any takers.

Similarly, another campground we looked at had a ridiculously steep price because the owners had spent lavishly to build themselves a seven-bedroom house. The new buyer, they reasoned, should repay them for that outlay—even though that bumped their asking price to nose-bleed levels. And who was going to want a seven-bedroom house, anyway?

And then there was the campground owner who let me know he'd bought his property for $1.6 million, when despite annual revenues of more than $500,000 it had been losing $150,000 a year. Seeing an opportunity to make money by slashing expenses, he'd promptly dropped the campground's KOA franchise and laid off his employees, optimistically deciding he could operate a 40-acre park with 150 sites and 20 cabins by himself, while his wife ran the store and took reservations. By the time I visited, seven years later, the only campground amenity in reasonably good repair was the swimming pool: one of the two bathhouses was essentially unusable, the water slide was completely overgrown and fenced-off, graffiti adorned several cabins, the enclosed pavilion was a shambles and the putt-putt course was a tangle of weeds and broken branches.

Asking price for this fixer-upper? $1.6 million, the owner said—even though gross annual revenues each of the previous two years had dropped to $170,000. After all, he patiently explained, he couldn't very well be expected to sell the place for less than he'd paid.

While such unrealistic expectations might be chalked up to naivete among sellers who were trying to market their properties themselves, we ran into them just as frequently among campgrounds being represented by brokers. After a handful of such experiences, I asked one of the brokers with whom we were working why he allowed his clients to waste my time and theirs in this manner. "I have to be careful how I phrase this," he responded. "We do spend a good deal of time trying to get the sellers to ask a reasonable price for their properties, but it's a struggle. But you're correct—I end up wasting a good deal of time presenting offers that will never fly, and I appreciate the position that puts you in."

My "position" was simply that a diligent broker wouldn't leave it up to the marketplace to educate his clients—that should be his job. But many brokers, I soon learned, were lazy at best and walking a fine ethical line at worst.

Most broker listings give only the most general description of where a campground is located, such as saying it's "somewhere in West Virginia" or "within a two-hour drive of a major metropolitan area," apparently to prevent interested buyers from contacting the seller directly. This attempt at secrecy extends even to pixelating identifying features on pictures of the property, such as entrance signs, creating a fun game for prospective buyers trying to see if they can outwit the broker's efforts to disguise a campground's location. Prospective buyers responding to the listings are then required to sign confidentiality statements, and once they're scheduled for a campground visit are warned that the one thing they must not do is let anyone know the campground is for sale.

This lack of transparency is explained as necessary to prevent either employees or seasonal campers from jumping ship—that once they learn an existing owner is trying to sell, anyone else

with a long-term investment in the property may likewise conclude it's time to leave.* But the insistence on controlling the sell-
er-buyer relationship can produce some strange contortions. How,
after all, could a prospective buyer examine a property without
prompting questions from either long-term campers or employees? In some cases I would tell the desk staff that I was looking for
an appropriate venue for a large family reunion, which give me a
reason for walking the property to look at RV sites and cabins, as
well as bathhouses and common facilities like pavilions or a swimming pool. But that didn't give me access to support facilities, like
the maintenance area or the office itself, so an alternative ploy I
adopted on a couple of occasions was to claim I was an insurance
adjuster—a risky gambit, since I know nothing about insurance
adjusting, but one that gave me an entree to just about anything I
wanted to see.

   As I quickly learned, however, the word was usually out,
anyway—unless I was the only prospective buyer, how many "insurance adjusters" or other nosy intruders could show up before
the jig was up, especially in a campground with a large percentage of seasonals? Walking into an RV park with a significant resident population is like walking into a small town: everyone knows
you're there, and most everyone knows why.

   While most brokers are just trying to protect their com-
missions—which can be as high as 5% to 7% on sales that run
into seven figures—the tendency toward secretiveness can also encourage less ethical behavior. For the seller, who typically is on the
hook for the entire commission, working a deal that cuts out the
broker can yield a significant savings. This was driven home to me
after I met with one campground owner for more than an hour
before the broker showed up, delayed by traffic, and then flew into

---

* There may be some truth to that, albeit rarely. We learned, for example, of a
nudist campground in Florida that was about to become a KOA franchise in 2013.
The owner was in an absolute panic that word not leak out until the last possible
moment— not because he'd lose customers, but because he was afraid his employees would quit once they learned they'd have to wear clothes to work.

a rage that we had spent all that time talking "behind his back." Meanwhile, with most campground sales executed by only one broker working both sides of the transaction and a huge payday riding on the outcome, the potential for mischief is obvious.

One of the brokers who showed us several New England properties that I thought were in our price range nevertheless kept urging me to look at a campground listed at more than $4 million—easily twice the amount I was considering— primarily because it had three housing units. Although the idea of having a separate home for each of our three couples was tempting, there wasn't any way I could come up with a million dollars to make the standard 25% down payment. But when I mentioned this to him, he brushed my concerns away.

"Don't worry," he reassured me. "I know a banker I've been working with for years who will get you in with just 10% down." Which sounded seductive, until I realized that 10% down would leave me with a $3.6 million debt, which at 6% interest over 20 years (standard rates at that time) would mean a monthly mortgage of just under $26,000. And that was for a Maine campground that was closed six months of each year, which meant I'd have to have another $156,000 in reserves just to get through the first winter.

That broker and I parted ways soon after.

The 2013 flood that overtopped our dam and inundated the walnut grove.

3. Sometimes, it is just skin deep

EIGHTEEN MONTHS and several thousand miles after embarking on a nationwide search for a campground, we ended up almost where we'd started, just a 90-minute drive from our home in northern Virginia.

In that time, we'd personally seen at least two dozen campgrounds between northern Maine and South Carolina—a handful more than once—and reviewed several dozen more on-line. Four of them we'd thought seriously about buying. One, visited in the dead of winter in central Ohio in our pre-fracking days, was grabbed by someone more nimble than us. A second, in central Virginia, we finally rejected because of access issues: half-a-mile of entrance road that was being pounded to death by logging trucks, plus an ungated railroad crossing. And two others, as already mentioned, where the owners proved emotionally unready to let go.

Along the way, we saw some real horror shows. One New England campground featured an amazing split-log main building that would have fit right in with the old Fred Harvey hotels of the National Park System, including a two-story balconied lobby and cathedral ceilings; unfortunately, the rest of the property dropped down to a river that flooded so frequently and so high that all the electrical cabling for the RV sites was strung from tree to tree, four to six feet off the ground. A New Jersey campground was so dominated by seasonal campers that one had nailed a "Private Property" sign to a tree at his site. A Kentucky campground had the misfortune of being in a dry county even as it featured a large concrete bunker in which campers would shelter when tornado sirens started wailing—which happened with some frequency, we learned, and surely was a time when adult beverages would be most in demand.

So when we finally submitted an offer on the Staunton/ Walnut Hills KOA, the few problems we saw were comparatively minor blemishes on an otherwise lovely piece of land. Opened in 1969 on the site of an old walnut plantation, the campground office and store were housed in a former stable built in the mid-18th century; in our years there, I would delight in showing campers the pegged post-and-beam construction and the remaining horse troughs, now repurposed for DVD and games storage. Two meandering creeks cut across the grounds and converged on a small three-acre lake, and with at least a third of the rolling grounds carpeted with lawn, the property readily earned its RV "park" designation.

With 126 RV sites, 11 tent sites and 13 cabins, the campground was large enough to generate enough revenue for all of us to live on. And its numerous amenities—including two bathhouses and a dump station, a game room, an enclosed pavilion, and a recently refurbished swimming pool—provided enough infrastructure to satisfy most campers' needs. The only immediately obvious drawback was the available on-site housing, which consisted of two double-wide trailers, requiring our two daughters and their husbands to share one roof.

Moreover, the double-wides were . . . well, trailers. The newer unit was next to the office and in relatively decent shape, but there was no getting around the inherent deficiencies of a "house" assembled with fiberboard walls and staple guns. Mice would invade us every winter, finding access through the myriad existing gaps for water lines and electrical conduits or making their own entrance points, setting off an annual and largely ineffective battle with traps and other deterrents. The living room floor underneath the wall-to-wall carpeting had an inexplicable wave, so that crossing the room was like walking on a ship's deck at sea, and I realized late one afternoon that I could see sunlight through the west-facing end wall, where the two halves of the unit weren't evenly matched and only the translucent siding kept out the elements. It wasn't long before Carin started referring to this as our "vinyl palace."

But the vinyl palace, alas, was head and shoulders above the other double-wide, a run-down unit of indeterminate age. Known as the Walnut House because of the color of its siding, it had been occupied for several years by a handicapped woman who smoked heavily and owned several large dogs. The combination was toxic: nicotine-saturated walls, stained and torn carpeting, scratched woodwork and smoky windowpanes that rattled in their sashes. As they surveyed their future home, I could see my daughters' spirits go into a nose-dive. Don't worry, I assured them. We'll take care of it.

Although closing on the campground was set for the end of January, we got the owner's permission to start renovations a month earlier. So, right after New Year's Day my older son-in-law, Mitch, and I moved into one of the "deluxe" cabins, rented a construction dumpster and went to work with hammers, crowbars and saws. First to go was the urine-stained carpeting, followed by the walls, which we ripped down to the studs. We pulled out all the single-paned windows, all the kitchen counters and cabinets and all the plumbing fixtures—learning, in the process, that the drain from the bathtub off the master bedroom had never been hooked up and had been discharging its contents directly onto the ground. When done, all we had left was an external shell with doors but no windows and a maze of wall studs, some of which we then moved or tore out altogether to create a floor plan better suited for two couples.

Along the way we discovered that a lot of the things we were trashing couldn't be replaced by a trip to the local Home Depot: house trailers, it turns out, have different standard sizes for windows, doors, and bathtubs, among other components. So while we awaited replacements, ordered from a specialized warehouse in Texas, we replaced sections of rotted-out subflooring, insulated the outside walls and some of those inside (for sound control), put up sheetrock and replaced flimsy trailer light switches and outlets with standard household fittings. As plumbing fixtures arrived, we put in new bathtubs, sinks and toilets, installed double-paned windows, hung new inside doors and put down hardwood floors. The finishing touch was to have Lowe's install new counters, cabinets, and kitchen appliances—and just like that, some $50,000 or more later, we had ourselves a solid second home that put the vinyl palace to shame.

Delighted as we all were with the outcome, however, we failed to recognize that our experience with the Walnut House should have been a warning of what lay ahead. The Walnut House's warts were obvious; the campground's deeper flaws and vulnerabilities were less so, concealed by its comely appearance and destined to erupt only at the most inopportune moments.

Many of the issues we encountered were unavoidably part of operating a business so intimately linked to the natural elements. Those ancient walnut trees that shade the oldest section of the campground? All well and good—until the fall, when camping beneath their canopy can resemble a bivouac in a hailstorm, ripe walnuts bouncing off aluminum and fiberglass roofs like gunshots. Those maples shading the hilltop pull-thru sites? An oasis in the heat of summer, but a deadly artillery range the winter we had a massive ice storm, with snapped limbs literally spearing one trailer and creating an impassable tangle of shattered branches that took days to clear. Those pretty creeks meandering among the RV and tent sites under the sycamore and catalpa trees? A great place to splash around on a hot summer day—until the thunderheads that piled up on those hot days would spill their contents, dropping several inches of rain in a torrent that overtopped the creeks and inundated our camp sites.

Our first spring we spent more than $7,000 for gravel to re-level the RV pads in the walnut grove, only to see it all wash away a few weeks later when we got slammed by an hours-long downpour. The creeks rose so high our inner roads were submerged, and everything constructed of wood that wasn't nailed down—landscape timbers, picnic tables, three foot-bridges—got swept into the lake. The lake, in turn, was so full it over-topped the earthen dam, eroding parts of the road that runs along its top, and one of the bridges washed over the dam and later had to be hauled out by a tractor. Seven thousand dollars in gravel? All gone as well, although some can still be seen on the downstream side of the dam.

That first shocking flood—we had several more in the years that followed, although none quite as severe—was a gut punch that taught me something emotionally I had previously appreciated only in the abstract: that nothing is all one thing, all good or all bad. Everything has a drawback to offset every advantage, a minus to balance each plus. Focus only on the positive and you're likely to get sucker-punched by the negative; see only the worst, and you're likely to be blinded to the best.

The lake itself was a prime example of this tension, and a constant reminder of the tradeoffs we had to accept. The visual focal point for the entire campground, its adjacent sites are some of the most sought-after in the park and its banks are frequently lined by campers fishing for perch, bluegill or large-mouth bass, the latter running to seven pounds or more. Heron, ospreys, and an occasional bald eagle fish the lake as well, and one year we even had a young beaver mosey through, felling one tree before he decided (thankfully!) to keep moving on. A bulletin board in the office registration area is covered with photos of happy campers proudly showing off their catch, with the biggest fish seemingly caught by the youngest people.

But the lake also is home to snapping turtles that in some cases have grown bigger than a garbage can lid, accounting to some extent for the rise and fall of the resident duck population. And thanks to the liberal use of fertilizer on the surrounding farms, drained by the two creeks that feed the lake, we waged a constant battle against algae that at times covered as much as half of the lake surface.*

We also had to combat an annual incursion of Canada geese. Once a protected migratory bird whose flights signaled the changing seasons, the species in recent decades has bifurcated, with one branch continuing to make the long haul from the northernmost reaches of Canada to as far south as Florida and Texas—but with another, apparently lazier cohort deciding no, what's the point of all that flying if we can just stay year-round in the Goldilocks middle of the continent? In the process, these winged symbols of freedom reveal themselves for what they really are, which is aggressive pooping machines, each producing up to two pounds of particularly slimy excrement every day that fouls waterways and seeds lawns with green land mines.

Once established, Canada geese can be nearly impossible to dislodge; one of the previous campground owners had been so overrun he eventually had to hire professional trappers to remove a gaggle that had moved in. If we were to avoid a repeat, we realized we had to jump on the first sign of an infestation, harassing the geese to such an extent that they'd move on before they got too comfortable. The problem was in figuring out how to sufficiently aggravate a 10-pound bird with a

---

*Throughout this text I refer to a body of water many others describe as a "pond," apparently in the belief that the difference between a lake and a pond is a matter of size—although just how big a pond must be before it qualifies as a lake is never explained. In my perhaps pedantic view, a pond is precisely that: a body of water that "ponds" and has nowhere to go except through evaporation or by sinking into the ground. The lake at Walnut Hills, small as it is, has both an inlet and an outlet and its waters move along quite energetically.

six-foot wing span that generally isn't intimidated by people.

One possibility, we soon learned from another camp-ground owner, was to get one or more swans with clipped wings. Swans apparently despise geese as much as we did and will readily attack them, while leaving ducks and other fowl unmolested, and the clipped wings keep them from flying off. Yet as attractive as the thought was of having our very own avian patrol to chase away our Canadian invaders, we wondered if we wouldn't be exchanging one problem for another: how would swans, a more aggressive spe-cies of fowl than our lovable ducks, interact with the kids and dogs that thronged the lake's banks? What would happen to them in winter? Hadn't we seen enough unintended consequences result-ing from people trying to control one environmental imbalance by introducing another? No, this would require direct action.

The first remedy we turned to was paintball guns, a non-lethal yet sufficiently painful—as any unarmored veteran of paint-ball wars can attest—way of delivering the message we wanted to convey. And, indeed, we had some initial success, until the geese learned to move out of range into the middle of the lake as soon as they saw us coming. More significantly, we had failed to anticipate that the sight of campground personnel patrolling the lake with any kind of gun would cause no small amount of consternation among our campers, a couple of whom ended up complaining to local wildlife authorities and bringing us unwanted uniformed visitors. There had to be a better way, and as with so many things today, the internet led us to it: laser pointers.

I have no idea why a laser dot on the water moving toward a Canada goose will freak it out, while eliciting only a duck equiv-alent of a yawn from a mallard, but that's exactly what happens. And so each evening in April and into May, whenever a honking gaggle of Canada geese would signal their imminent arrival, we'd be ready with our light sabers and would make their lives hell until they gave up. Sometimes it took only a few minutes, and after a few repeated forays they'd move on—until the next year.

But the lake posed other challenges. The combination of

snapping turtles and algae was sufficient explanation for why we prohibited campers from entering the lake, but there was another, less readily visible problem that made swimming impractical: the basin was filling up. Created roughly 30 years earlier through a combination of excavation and dam building, Lake Kerplonken—as it was playfully dubbed by a previous owner's youthful relative—was originally eight feet deep for virtually its entire length and width. Decades of run-off, however, had filled it up with so much silt that the inlet was no more than a couple of feet deep and the dam end wasn't much better, and with each passing year the water overall got more and more shallow. Eventually we were going to end up with a marsh.

In 2018, as mud bars began emerging at the shallow end, we hired an engineering firm to conduct a bathymetric survey so we could find out just how much silt had accumulated. The sobering answer: more than 13,000 cubic yards, or enough to cover a football field to a height of almost nine feet.

Getting rid of the stuff, we soon learned, was not going to be either cheap or easy, although clearly something had to be done. One alternative, suggested by several campground owners with whom we shared our plight, would be to finish what nature had started by draining the lake, trucking in tons of additional fill and converting the three-acre expanse into a meadow—incidentally creating room for many more RV sites, they pointed out, with "let's make lemonade from lemons" enthusiasm. But that "solution," practical though it might have been, just made us blanch.

Instead, we took out a six-figure loan to underwrite what we envisioned as the first of three dredging operations, to be spread out over several years. Money—or the lack of it—was certainly one reason for the staggered approach, but we also had to deal with issues of time and space: the barge-based project couldn't start until peak season ended, in early November, and would have to wrap up when winter kicked in hard, usually by mid-December. And whatever was sucked out of the lake within that six-week window would have to be pumped into dewatering bags and left for several months, until it had drained enough to be scooped up and hauled off in dump trucks.

In the end, we finished 2018 with more than 4,000 cubic yards of muck packed into huge polypropylene tubes, each six feet in diameter and 100 feet long, covering all of one road and entirely blocking the north side of the lake. There it sat until March, an impressive wall of bagged mud—until one realized that there was twice as much of it still in the lake, with more flowing in with every rainfall.

While our ongoing struggles with Lake Kerplonken were an extreme example of the liabilities side of the environmental balance sheet, we also learned that the human ledger has its own hidden costs. Some of those costs were undiscernible because we were new to the business, and so hadn't yet learned the kinds of maintenance issues that any aging infrastructure will have; some were the inevitable result of an evolving industry that keeps generating new demands, such as the ever-growing thirst for more electricity. But some were simply the result of past work that had been done on the quick and cheap—a problem not unique to Walnut Hills, but endemic to an industry that for decades had skated on the edge of profitability and was run by "can-do" types, even when they couldn't.

The prime example in that regard was our waterworks. While some campgrounds are lucky enough to have access to municipal water and sewer services, most—almost by definition— are in non-urbanized areas and rely on private wells and septic systems. We were fortunate in that our campground's only well was a solid producer that has for decades reliably supplied water to all 137 RV and tent sites plus nine of our 13 cabins, two bathhouses, two residences and the store. But to reach its end-users that water must flow through a series of plastic pipes and valves, all of which were installed by past property owners short on cash, and perhaps short on skilled labor as well.

Not long after we bought Walnut Hills we sprang our first leak, and from that point averaged probably one a month. The initial tip-off would be a lightbulb mounted outside the pump house door, visible from the office, that came on every time the pump was running. Normally the bulb would stay lit for a couple of minutes, but when it never turned off or cycled back on after less than a minute, we knew it was time to start walking the park in search of soggy ground, pooling water or, with really bad breaks, a man-made spring bubbling to the surface.

Then the digging would start, preferably with a shovel but in extreme cases—when the ground was especially rocky or the water line especially deep—a backhoe. The tricky part of using mechanized equipment, however, was that we never knew what else we might hit. We had no plat maps to show us where utilities were buried—just one of the handicaps faced by most decades-old campgrounds—and as we soon learned, none of the electrical cable had been run through conduit, making it vulnerable to nicks and cuts from careless digging. To make matters worse, the power lines often had been buried in the same trench as the water line, while also crisscrossing the grounds were television cables, sewer pipes and a web of long-defunct telephone lines that had serviced every site before the ubiquity of cell phones.

We also soon discovered that none of the campground's waterline trenches had been prepped with gravel beds: plastic water pipe had simply been dropped into the dirt and then covered with the excavated fill. Heaved by frost and compressed by massive RVs rolling above, the dirt and rocks had for years rubbed against polyethylene embrittled by the chlorine used as a disinfectant, eventually creating first a crack and then a split. Moreover, it didn't help that virtually all the pipe we encountered was of the thin-walled variety. Thick-walled would have been more durable, of course—but it's stiffer and harder to work. And, most critically, it's more expensive.

The upper bathhouse was another example of cutting corners for short-term gain but long-term headaches. Although built only a few years earlier, in an area that had the campground's largest concentration of seasonal sites and all of its primitive cabins and tent sites, the bathhouse inexplicably was uninsulated and unheated and therefore had to be closed each winter. Doubtless someone had reasoned that seasonal campers could use their own on-board showers—although many would prefer otherwise, because of the small size of RV hot-water heaters— but they still had to trek down a steep hill to the lower bathhouse to do laundry. And campers renting one of the primitive cabins, not to mention the occasional winter tent camper, had an even longer trek to the lower bathhouse to use a toilet or to wash their dishes, never mind showers and laundry.

One of our first projects, therefore, was to put in a heating system and to have insulation blown into the walls so the bathhouse could remain open year-round. This was an imperfect solution, however, because many of the water pipes ran inside external walls, and even with the new insulation were inadequately protected against winter temperatures that could easily drop into the single digits. So for the first couple of years we had to contend with an occasional burst pipe until we figured out where the weak spots were, adding heat tape or baseboard heaters to prevent a recurrence.[*]

These and other problems were only minimally visible to our campers, even as they kept us scrambling. But one problem we couldn't mitigate, and that increasingly became a sore point for campers that they didn't hesitate to complain about, was our wi-fi service—an example not of shoddy workmanship or of tight-fisted spending, but of rising customer expectations bumping against circumstances completely beyond the campground's control.

By now it's an industry standard that wi-fi is a campground's fourth utility, after water and electricity and sometimes ahead of sewer. But that's a relatively new development, and in 2013 Walnut Hills had been limping along for several years with no more than one T-1 line servicing the entire campground's in-

---

[*]More proof of how poorly this bathhouse was conceived and built was discovered when we sold the campground, when a building inspector found that the foundation was cracking and the entire structure—built into the side of a slope—was in danger of collapsing. That turned out to be a $25,000 stabilization project.

ternet needs. Without getting bogged down in jargon, suffice to say that T-1 is a telephone line with extremely limited capacity by today's standards, with barely enough internet bandwidth for our business needs, much less for a campground with 150 sites and easily twice that number of people trying to get on-line.

Small wonder, then, that as a growing number of campers arrived with laptops and tablets and cell phones, expecting not only to check their email but to stream movies and play games online, the complaints started pouring in. Things got so bad that we created a handout for the front desk to explain our limitations, under the bold headline, "It's true—our wi-fi is crap!"—a line cribbed from a note dropped into our suggestion box by an irate camper.

Finding an alternative to T-1 lines, however, was no easy task. Satellite service was one possibility, but such links tend to be the channels of last resort for truly remote customers because of upload and download time lags. Microwave transmission was another, albeit hobbled by line-of-sight difficulties in Virginia's hilly terrain. That left cable—but the only cable provider in our area was Comcast, which wanted to charge us $12 a foot to trench from our property to its nearest service point, roughly a mile away. Somehow, I just couldn't stomach (or afford!) contributing $55,000 to Comcast's capital improvements budget, and so there matters stood for a couple of years.

Comcast, however, had a problem that eventually played in our favor: it's so big that its left hand doesn't know what its right hand is doing. Its marketing department had decided that we should get periodic notifications that we "qualified" for their internet and cable service, and every time I replied to one of their mailings with a "Yes, I'm interested, tell me more!" response, someone in their engineering department would be assigned to assess our situation. Eventually I'd be given the exciting news that a mere $55,000 separated our campground from the digital age, which I would ignore, and after a couple of months I'd get another breathless come-on. I'd respond as I had before and the whole process would repeat, and then repeat again, our very own version of the movie "Groundhog Day."

After two years of this two-step, I unexpectedly got a phone call from a Comcast representative located in . . . Maine, of all places. After 30 years with the company, Dan said, he was the one to whom Comcast gave the "problem" cases, which apparently we had become. Comcast's engineers were complaining that they kept being assigned to evaluate Walnut Hills for cable service, but each time they did a survey the results were always the same. Why was I sending so many requests for service and then not following through?

"Well, Dan," I answered. "You guys keep telling me that I've been qualified to get internet and cable, but when I express an interest in signing up, Comcast tells me we're good to go— just as soon as I come up with $55,000 to get started. I don't know what 'qualified' means to you, but to me that's like saying I'm qualified for the Olympics just as soon as I run a 4-minute mile. Not going to happen."

Dan was silent for a long moment. "Okay," he finally said. "Let's take a closer look."

Thus began an hour-long conversation—the first time anyone from Comcast had actually talked to me—in which Dan had me describe the property, pored over satellite images, and pulled up county records, including the GIS mapping survey. "What's this narrow green band running diagonally across part of the campground?" he eventually asked, referring to a copy of the site map that I had scanned and emailed to him while we talked.

"That's the power line right-of-way," I said.

"Any reason why we can't string the Comcast cable along those poles?"

"I don't know, Dan. That certainly seems feasible to me, and I'm sure would be a whole lot cheaper than digging a mile-long trench, but I'm not an engineer."

"Engineers!" he responded impatiently. "All they think about is digging."

After that, it still took another six months for all the piec-es to fall into place, a process complicated by the fact that two utilities now had to coordinate their efforts. But by Christmas of 2015 we had two 100-megabit lines servicing the campground, at no installation cost to us, and Walnut Hills was plunged into the internet age. And just for good measure, all our neighbors now had access to fast internet, too.

Oops. Too much coach, not enough driver.

4. The customer is not always right

FOR ALL OUR MANY MONTHS of self-education and preparation
as future campground operators, there remained a huge blind spot
that I wasn't aware existed until we were in the middle of it—and
boy, was it a doozy.

We had, after all, backgrounded ourselves as thoroughly as
I thought possible. Picking up on several leads from our training
seminar with Darrell Hess, I had become an associate member of
ARVC, the nation's only campground trade association. Months
before we owned a campground I attended a week-long ARVC
workshop attended by several dozen representatives of every imag-
inable kind of camping facility, from private to public to Corps
of Engineers to Native American, of all ages and levels of experience. We exchanged personal histories, listened to lectures and
role-played various scenarios.

Some of the latter should have tipped me off, but really—how realistic was it that campers would deliberately poop in
the swimming pool? Or smear feces on bathroom walls? Was that

even a thing?*

Mitch, my son-in-law, and I also attended our first ARVC convention, held in late 2012 in Las Vegas. There we attended more seminars, schmoozed with other campground owners, played the slots and didn't realize that a bigger gamble was awaiting us back in Virginia, where we were in serious negotiations to buy Walnut Hills. We talked maintenance issues, ownership structures, environmental challenges, social media, advertising and promotion, and on and on and I still didn't get it.

Years later, I encountered an aphorism that perfectly summarized what I'd been missing: "Hospitality means making your guests feel at home, even when you wish they were."

"Guests." The people who were missing from my calculus. The people who came rolling into our campground in everything from a beat-up old camper that literally had its roof held down with duct tape (true story!) to half-million-dollar motor coaches towing 30- and 40-foot trailers crammed with canoes, ATVs, dirt bikes and any kind of grown-up toy you could imagine. People who had never been in an RV before but were too embarrassed to ask for help, and people who'd been camping for decades and knew everything, even when they didn't. People who would ask permission to do the most innocuous things for fear of assuming too much, and people who ignored all the rules because—well, because they were out to have a good time. And they weren't home. And somebody else would clean up the mess—right?

Guests were a lot of work. Guests had to be greeted with a smile and have their problems resolved smoothly and compassionately, regardless of how much they made me want to scream.

---

*FYI: yes, it is. So is the amount of time campground owners spend talking to each other about every possible bathroom subject, often over a meal. Big topics include the trend toward "family-type" bathrooms, which have a cluster of individual rooms rather than the more common group facilities and which often are preferred by families—as well as by teenage couples who may inadvertently start one; and the unfortunate use of so-called "flushable" wipes, which are death on septic systems. If you want to get a campground owner into an animated discussion, just bring up the latter topic.

One problem we quickly recognized is that campers are not a monolithic bunch. They're all over the map in their ideas about what it means to go camping, from those for whom it's all about nature and escaping from the suffocating, technologically driven world they live in, to those for whom it's about traveling in a smaller version of their homes, with all the comforts to which they'd grown accustomed. Some are looking for peace and quiet and a time for reflection; others are seeking a chance to cut loose and pa-a-a-r-ty. It all makes for a combustible mix, yet all required us to be hospitable.*

Another problem is that campgrounds—much, I suspect, like restaurants—attract the know-it-alls who are only too happy to tell you what you should be doing differently. Sometimes this helpfulness would extend to the most banal prescriptions, such as, "You know, you really should think about adding sewer to those sites in the front of the campground." (What? Those sites don't have sewer?) At other times it was just dumb, as with the suggestion that it would be convenient if the dumpsters were moved from the campground entrance to the middle of the property—convenient, that is, only until the first time the garbage trucks rolled in at 5 a.m. and started banging around. Eventually we compiled a list of the most frequently made "suggestions," restating them as questions with our answers, and distributed the resulting three-page FAQ at the front desk.

Yet another problem—and perhaps the one that should lead the list—was the campers who arrived with their own definite ideas about what our services were worth and how much they should pay for them. Some demanded *a la carte* pricing, because why should they pay for a swimming pool they wouldn't be using

---

*Nor does the public-at-large have a common understanding of what a campground is all about. Several times we had a small fleet of "green" school buses pull in, en route from a manufacturing plant in the Carolinas to the New England schools that were buying them, seeking to refill their propane tanks. We were happy to sell them the propane, of course, but not so happy that they were clogging our driveway as our paying customers were trying to register.

or wi-fi they didn't need;[*] others bristled at being charged for additional accommodations, whether it was for more than two cars or four people on a site, or for visitors staying more than two hours, which were our baselines. And discounts were a big thing, perhaps because so many campgrounds offer them willy-nilly—and jack up their prices accordingly, which creates resentment among campers who inadvertently pay full freight. The only discounts we ever offered was for a KOA Value Kard (initially) or for Good Sam memberships (later), reasoning that offering the full smorgasbord would devalue the membership cards we *were* honoring and for which our campers had paid. But no matter how clearly we articulated our position, the questions would come volleying back: what about Passport America? Military or police? *Active* military? No? Then how about senior citizens? Triple A?

One young man, checking in with his Mennonite family, grew almost indignant when I rejected his request for a discount. "Why should we give you a discount?" I asked, intrigued.

"Because we do good works!" he answered, apparently oblivious to how that came across.

Early on, I learned not to get into discussions about military discounts, which almost always ended badly. In my view, while some active military personnel may have been in front-line positions that deserved an "attaboy" from us, the great majority either were desk jockeys or grease monkeys doing a job like anyone else or had been retired for the past 20 years. I could see giving a break to those who were actively putting their lives on the line, but by the same logic I should do likewise for cops and other first responders—and inner-city schoolteachers and other civil servants in precarious situations. And why draw the line at "public" service? How about private-sector doctors and nurses, or electric company linemen, or any number of other dangerous or helping professions

---

[*]On the other hand, campgrounds that provide this kind of pricing structure often get slammed for "nickle-and-diming" their customers by having so many separate charges. Apparently there's no winning this one.

that contribute to the general welfare?

Most military folks would simply reply "Oh, okay," when I told them we didn't offer a military discount, but there was an entitled segment that apparently felt they'd earned a lifetime pass from the private sector. After trying to explain our position to a couple of veterans who challenged me on the issue, to their vast irritation— and possibly contempt—I just stopped trying to justify myself.

Along with expecting every courtesy from us, an astonishing number of people seemingly expected none from themselves. I was repeatedly surprised by how many parents were oblivious to the tidal wave of noise generated by their children as they raced around our little store, drowning out the customers who were trying to conduct business with our desk clerks. Or the people who would park in front of the door, engine running, completely blocking the campground exit while they poked around our shelves for several minutes. Almost anyone can be hospitable to polite, cheerful and responsive people, but this subset of humanity tested the limits.

And then there were the people—thankfully rather limited in number—who can only be described as weird. And in some of those cases, I must admit, my sense of hospitality utterly failed.

One particularly busy Sunday, as a steady stream of RVs was exiting the campground, I stood across from the office, playing goodwill ambassador by waving good-bye to the departures. A black pickup truck pulling a travel trailer stopped in front of me. The driver got out, went around to the back, and without saying a word pulled out a bag of trash from the pickup bed—which he then dropped onto the ground next to the late-arrival kiosk.

"Sir," I called out, "please don't drop your trash there!"

"I didn't know where else to put it," he replied, heading back to his cab.

"You could have left it at your site for us to pick up," I replied, "but you'll be passing a dumpster at the exit as you head out." No answer.

As the cab door swung shut and the pick-up started rolling, I stepped forward, picked up the bag and tossed it back into the pickup bed. The driver stopped. To my amazement, he hopped back out, grabbed the bag and dropped it back on the ground in the same spot as before. As he got back into the cab, I shook my head. "Sir," I said, "this isn't a trash heap. I'd appreciate it if you'd dispose of your trash appropriately. You'll be driving right past the dumpster on your way out."

No response. The truck started moving. I once again bent down, lifted the bag and tossed it into the back. Truck stopped. Driver got out, grabbed the bag and this time threw it to the ground for emphasis.

By now I wasn't even angry anymore. The situation was so crazy it had tipped into farce, and I found myself wondering when the camper would realize he could never drive away fast enough to escape the trash bag I was going to toss back into his vehicle. "You know," I said, as I returned the bag to his truck yet again, "there's no way you can win this one."

He glared, but this time drove away. But when he stopped at the dumpster, I saw that it was his wife who got out to properly dispose of the garbage.

According to prevailing views of hospitality, I probably should have taken that bag to the dumpster myself and not made an issue out of it—but that would have rewarded bad behavior, and there already was too much of that going around. Yet this encounter encapsulated one of the hardest challenges with which I wrestled throughout our eight years, of finding the right balance between enforcing our rules (or even rules of common courtesy) and cutting our customers some slack because they were ignorant and didn't know any better, or because they were tired and not thinking clearly. I know there were times when I failed. And almost inevitably, when I did I could expect to read an online review a day or two later blasting the "angry old white-haired guy."

Still, I had to wonder at people who acted as if they owned the place. Like the guy who apparently had no qualms about telling one of our maintenance men to stop mowing because he was worried that the paint job on his motorcoach might get dinged by a flying rock. As I told him, barely able to control my temper, he may or may not have had a legitimate concern, but until he started signing my employees' paychecks he was in no position to issue them orders and should address his concerns to me. Or like the guy I flagged down driving the wrong way on one of our narrow one-way roads, despite an unavoidable "do not enter" sign, because it was a more direct route to his site and was going to save him a few minutes. "It's okay—I'm a cop," he assured me, as my jaw dropped. "You, of all people, should know better," I finally replied.

People's capacity for rationalizing, denying, or ignoring their own behavior never ceased to amaze me and always, always tested my patience. Every camper who checked in was given a site map, on the back of which was a list of our rules and regulations—rules and regulations that virtually no one read, my daughter assured me. She was right.[*] Yet even the two rules we stressed verbally at check-in were reliably ignored: please always observe the 10 miles-per-hour speed limit, and please don't park or drive on the grass anywhere in the park. Most campers would take that to heart, but a stubborn few would ignore waddling ducks, kids on bicycles and old folks out for a stroll as they zipped around on our gravel roads, a rooster-tail of dust hanging in their wake. Stop them to ask that they slow down, and they'd swear they hadn't been going too fast, that they'd had an eye on the speedometer the whole time, all evidence to the contrary.

The plea to keep vehicles off the grass, meanwhile, was one of our biggest headaches, exacerbated by three factors. One, because of the age of the campground, quite a few sites had gravel pads that were too short for both a tow vehicle and the ever-longer trailers and fifth-wheels that have become more common. While

---

[*]One indication that she was right: the very last "rule" was a ban on vampires and werewolves anywhere on the grounds, with a request that the office be notified if the rule were violated. Perhaps all of half-a-dozen guests remarked on it during our eight years, suggesting that the vast majority never read that far.

in all such cases we had additional parking available within 200 feet, some campers simply insisted on crowding everything into their site, leading to the inescapable erosion of pad and site boundaries.

A second problem was a growing trend toward campers arriving with more than one vehicle, and while many sites could accommodate two cars or pick-up trucks, there were none that could fit three or four. Again, there always was nearby parking available—but why walk a hundred feet from your car when you could park it on the grass right next to your trailer? So what if the campground began to resemble a parking lot? Getting people to move their excess vehicles to a more suitable area was a constant battle of wills, a source of great anxiety for staff members tasked with enforcing the rules, and possibly our greatest source of online complaints about the campground.

The third problem was the soft ground. Every season we had people who didn't see any problem with driving onto a lawn because it made it easier for them to back into a site, or because they wanted to make a U-turn—until, that is, they realized they'd created furrows deep enough for planting crops. The combination of a high water table and the 6,000-pound weight of a travel trailer was enough to create an unsightly mess, but that paled in comparison to the damage a 30,000-pound motor coach could inflict. And some did.

It may be intuitively obvious to most people that driving a motorcoach or large fifth-wheel is significantly different from driving a car, but as the frequency with which our grass was torn up illustrated, an alarming number of campers were getting behind the wheel with little if any practice or understanding of what they were undertaking. The resulting mayhem, as often as not, would be blamed on the campground for having trees, fences, boulders and other obstacles in the wrong place. Operator error? Not a chance.

We had one camper pulling a fifth-wheel who on entering the park took a right turn too wide because he was afraid of hitting a tree on his passenger side. In doing so, his tail end swung too far left and clipped another tree, damaging the back end of his rig—and his pride. "That tree is too close to the road!" he yelled when I raced to the scene, overlooking the fact that every RV on the premises had made the exact same turn without hitting anything. He then ordered his wife and teenage son to get out of the rig, handed them each a walkie-talkie, and had them escort him to his site on foot, front and aft, talking him through every turn. He did the same when they left, and I doubt they ever returned.[*]

Our split-rail fences were a frequent target. One was in front of the vinyl palace, separating our double-wide from a visitor parking lot. It was not unusual for cars pulling into one of its spots to bump the fence, but on one occasion we had a teenage driver pull in so hard that he split one of the rails. He promptly took off, fleeing for the uncertain sanctuary of his parents' camping site, where I caught up with him and asked if he knew what he had done. He didn't deny it, but instead replied, "Well, it's your fault for having the fence there." A heated exchange was forestalled only because his father heard how his son was responding and tore into him for being a jerk, as well as apologizing to me.

A more extreme version of the same sort of thing happened when I asked a driver hauling a fifth-wheel to pull forward because he was blocking the entrance driveway. "Where do you want me to go?" he asked, with a belligerent tone. I pointed to a section of road alongside the fence next to the swimming pool and suggested that was a good spot to get out of the way, and he grudgingly moved. Moments later, his business in the store completed, he returned to his rig—and made such a sharp left turn that the back end of his fifth-wheel took out three fence posts and shattered several rails.

"Well, I was only parking where you told me to park!" he shouted, when I erupted in anger at his clumsiness.

---

[*] To be fair, this particular camper was not the first to hit that particular tree, as he was quick to observe by pointing to several scars on the trunk. Indeed, we probably had one or two inept drivers hit that tree each year—and after this incident we finally cut it down, although it pained me to do so. Another reward for bad behavior!

"I didn't tell you to knock down several sections of fence!"
I shouted back, in one of my less praise-worthy moments of customer hospitality.

While anything to do with maneuvering large pieces of
mechanized equipment was our number one source of headaches,
a close second was anything to do with firewood and fire rings.
While there is a small—although increasingly larger and more vo-
cal—segment of the camping public that objects to wood smoke,
the majority of campers still think of a campfire as a quintessential
element of the camping "experience." And in the same way that
the simple act of leaving home seems to create an "anything goes"
mentality for some campers, the opportunity to burn things is for
some an invitation to disregard common sense.

Campfires became bonfires, their flames licking six feet or
higher. Campers would start a fire in the afternoon, then leave
their sites unattended for several hours. The county burn ban, pro-
hibiting open fires before 4 p.m. each spring, became something
to argue about. Not our rule, we'd point out, stressing that both
they and we could be fined for failure to comply. In one case, after a group of campers repeatedly refused to douse their morning
fire— "We were just waiting for it to burn down," they explained
45 minutes later—I drove up in a golf car and swiftly poured a
bucket of water into the fire ring, leaving slack jaws hanging as I
drove way. That wasn't hospitable, I know.

One ongoing point of friction was our ban on bringing in
outside firewood. Such bans are widespread in the campground
industry, and particularly on public lands, and are a largely failed
effort to limit the spread of invasive insects and diseases that are
exterminating entire species of trees. Unevenly enforced and sometimes poorly explained, the bans are viewed by many campers as
nothing more than a campground trying to monopolize sales of
its own firewood—which is ironic, given that much of the wood
sold at Walnut Hills was from the campground's ash trees, all of
which had been killed by the emerald ash borer within the span of
a single year.

Oblivious to such concerns, campers arriving with a load of firewood created a public relations nightmare for us. Telling them they had to leave, which would have been optimal, was impractical. Explaining that they unwittingly could be transporting gypsy moths, which feast on oaks and aspens, or a fungus that is infecting walnut trees, was difficult and sometimes poorly received. The best we could do was ask that they not put any firewood on the ground and that they burn everything completely, but as the loss of our ash trees demonstrated, this was hardly sufficient.

Just as aggravating were the campers—usually but not exclusively tenters—who viewed our campground as "the woods," with anything they could pick up as fuel for their fire rings. Sometimes that would mean scavenging for downed limbs and branches, despite the prohibition in our rules against doing so; sometimes it would mean actually cutting down trees, by those who came prepared to do so. Indeed, the campground's previous owner recalled for us how one of his campers came equipped with a chainsaw, which he used with great abandon while other campers ignored him, thinking that surely someone with a chainsaw must be a Walnut Hills employee.

As I would patiently explain to the scavenging offenders, Walnut Hills had 18,000 camper nights a year and at most 15 acres of woods: that ratio would result in total deforestation within a couple of years if every one of those campers helped themselves to firewood for the night. What I didn't try to relate was that some wood scavengers were idiots who didn't know the difference between a dead tree and a living one, and green trees don't burn particularly well. Or that leaving a fire ring with half-burnt stumps and charred 10-foot limbs dragged out of the underbrush created a housekeeping nightmare for the maintenance crew after the campers departed. Or that there was something extraordinarily thoughtless and cruel about using a hatchet to lop off chunks of bark from living trees for "tinder," leaving the underlying cambium vulnerable to insects and rot, as was done by one group of young pioneers.

To be honest, contemplating such wanton destruction

sometimes wrung all the patience out of me. In one particular case, as I stood beside a tent and looked at a freshly cut stump near a fire ring in which laid a half-burnt sapling, its leaves curdled by the heat, I completely lost my shit and started yelling at the two sleeping women, jolting them awake. That little escapade got me a scathing on-line review, and to some extent deservedly so. It also prompted me to formulate a rule that we would start charging campers by the inch of trunk diameter for any tree they cut down, and after that such incidents became markedly fewer.

The treating of someone else's property as one's own, but without any of the responsibilities of ownership, was noticeably more prevalent among locals—people who lived within a 30-minute drive or so. I don't know whether it was the culture, or whether this was a phenomenon that could be attributed to familiarity breeding contempt, but more often than not any incidents of petty vandalism could be traced to someone local. Our cabins were especially hard-hit the first couple of years, not just by generally trashy behavior but because—as I slowly came to realize—they were viewed as convenient local spots for drug dealing and casual sex, activities that can be hard on the facilities. That's when we started charging up-front refundable cleaning fees and required anyone renting a cabin to be at least 21 and to provide us with a driver's license and credit card, and with that this problem diminished as well.

Also helping weed out the undesirables was a blacklist that we created midway through our first year, as we began to recognize certain repeat offenders. As we added names I would send a letter to the offenders, suggesting they would save themselves some embarrassment if they didn't try to book a return visit, and I don't think any of them tried to test the ban. Our first couple of years we added more than a hundred names to the list, but after that the tally dropped off sharply.

For much the same reason, after two years we ended my predecessor's practice of selling day-passes for use of the swimming pool—and saw a marked diminishment in the noise level, as well as in the amount of trash we had to clean up each evening. Instead, we instituted a seasonal pass for non-campers, and the difference between a $5 day pass and a $160 seasonal pass brought in an entirely different class of customers. Best of all, ending the day-passes also ended any incidents of poop in the pool—something that occurred once a year for the first two years and which, curiously, was reported to us each time with great indignation by the same boisterous family of day-pass users.

But the biggest—and completely unanticipated—test of our hospitality was posed by the homeless. These were not full-timers, who live in their RVs out of personal choice and may or may not be "houseless," but people who couldn't afford to rent a house or apartment and were looking for cheap alternatives. This group has grown steadily over the years, as the supply of affordable housing keeps shrinking, resulting in phone calls that typically would start with the question, "What's your monthly rate for cabins?"—a sure-fire tip-off that the caller wasn't just looking for a vacation spot. Since campground cabins are more expensive than a motel room, answering the question would usually be enough to end the conversation, but we instituted a one-week maximum rule for cabin occupancy anyway.

Less immediately overt were the tent campers who would rent a site for a few days, then start extending their stays, a night or two at a time. Pop-ups, as the cheapest of all RVs, also grew in popularity for prolonged stays by those without an established address, but neither tents nor pop-ups have a lot of living space, and even less so if there's a bunch of kids involved. Eventually the long-term nature of such situations would become inescapably manifest, as once-tidy sites began to overflow with coolers, cooking gear, dorm-size refrigerators, outdoor stoves, children's bicycles and other toys, lounging chairs in various states of disrepair, towels or sleeping bags tossed over a clothesline, and in one extreme case, a regular mattress. What had been a recreational camping spot thus would be transformed into a homeless encampment, and while we struggled with middle-class guilt about giving the boot to people obviously fallen on hard times, we had a business to protect and limits on our ability to solve housing dilemmas. We ended up extending the one-week limit to tents and pop-up campers, too.

In tandem with this phenomenon, it became obvious that others also started thinking of campgrounds as a resource for addressing problems they weren't equipped to handle. We had local social agencies that on several occasions rented a cabin or tent site for clients they didn't know where else to place, and while such placements were limited by our one-week maximum policy, the people in these circumstances typically would not have their own transportation. That left us with a captive population relying on frequently overwhelmed social providers for rides to get food, cigarettes or other necessities, and when that support didn't materialize, or was too infrequent, they'd turn to our paying guests with requests for help, panhandling or mooching food.

That was uncomfortable enough—but there were still darker problems with which we had to contend.

The result of poking at a wiring harness with a screwdriver.

5. A walk on the dark side

A COUPLE OF DECADES AGO, I dabbled in a computer game called Sim City, "sim" being short for "simulated." The idea was to build a city, putting housing developments here and stores and factories there, connecting everything with roads and bridges that spanned the pretty little river running down the middle of my idyllic community, and pretty soon people would start moving in and the place would come alive.

And the problems would start.

Building public infrastructure takes money, which means taxes, which inevitably leads to protests. Don't tax enough and things start to fall apart, and you also don't keep up with growth, which further accelerates infrastructure deterioration. Raise taxes to meet growing demand and your Sim City residents start protesting that they shouldn't have to pay for public schools because they don't have kids, or that only the people who actually use the public park should be footing the bill for its upkeep. Meanwhile, pressure mounts to put in public transit because traffic is becoming horrendous and the air is getting polluted, and there's mounting concern that your storm sewers are overwhelming the sewage treatment plant and flushing untreated human waste into that pretty little river and . . . .

For a "game," it was exhausting. It was also a lot like running a campground, which I soon realized was a lot like trying to run a small town. My days would start at 7 a.m. and continue non-stop until after dark, seven days a week, and meant skipping so many meals that within the first two years I dropped enough weight to get back into a pants size I'd last worn 40 years earlier. I would start the day with a "to-do" list of perhaps a dozen items, and 12 hours later would realize I hadn't made it even half-way through because of all the unexpected demands on my time that had popped up along the way. Some, like a water leak, would be an emergency; others weren't in the same category, but only if nipped in the bud. All needed immediate attention.

With 150 sites, including cabins and tents, there might be as many as 600 people at Walnut Hills on a busy weekend, each with their own demands and expectations and each carrying their own personal baggage. Most of the time they meshed okay, because most people were at the campground to have a good time and weren't looking for aggravation. But sometimes it wouldn't take much to tip things a bit too far, and sometimes real-world problems of a sort that no computer game has replicated would creep in.

An ostensibly lighter example of reality's curve balls was provided by Hero, the two-legged calf, who arrived at the campground in his own little trailer, accompanied by his owner in a more conventional fifth-wheel. Hero was on his way to a nearby farm that his owner had just acquired, but the facilities weren't quite ready and needed another couple of weeks for completion, so would it be possible for him to stay on one of our sites for that long? And oh, yes—his owner would need a site as well.

Did I mention that Hero had only two legs?

As his owner was quick to tell us—and as I soon learned, anyone else who would listen—Hero had been neglected by a former owner and had lost his back legs to severe frostbite, but his new owner had hooked up with a veterinary hospital at Texas A&M that was willing to fit him with a set of prosthetic limbs. Because calves grow up to be cows (or steers, in this case), the prosthetics had to be refitted as Hero grew bigger, and now Hero was returning from one of those adjustments and in need of a lay-over. Since it was early in the season and we still had a lot of room, I said sure, we could do that—provided that Hero's "deposits" were picked up promptly and that he didn't become a fly magnet.

I was assured that would be the case, and so for about two weeks Hero became a local sensation, following his owner on walks around the campground like a dog on a leash, much to the excited amusement of any kids on the grounds. A local television station did a feel-good feature about the plucky animal and his compassionate owner, adding to the wave of publicity that she had promoted ever since Hero's initial surgery, in 2013, including a spot on Dr. Phil. A series of four illustrated kids' books was launched, with half of the proceeds supposed to benefit an amputee youth camp in Knoxville, Tenn., and as recently as mid-2020 a three-minute clip of Hero's salvation was uploaded to the YouTube "OnlyGoodTV" channel.

Less publicly observed, however, was Hero's death in November 2016, or just three years after the publicity mill got cranking. The only mention of his demise appears to have been a Facebook post by the woman who wrote the first illustrated children's book—the rest of the series apparently never got published—which sold only a smattering of copies and generated a handful of vituperative reviews accusing the author of cashing in on "someone else's story." Ditto for Hero's rescuer, who after getting slammed on the internet for allegedly using Hero to pull at donors' heartstrings, vanished without a word of explanation about his death.

But at least the bleak conclusion to this episode occurred elsewhere. There would be enough dark clouds passing over Walnut Hills without the possibly shady exploitation of a benighted bovine.

There was, for example, the inexplicable desire for many campers to have a golf car* in which to toodle around the premises, even though a 10-minute walk would take them from one end of the grounds to the other. Quite a few would bring their own, sometimes loaded into the bed of a pick-up and sometimes pulled in an extra trailer, many of them dolled up with lots of chrome, mag wheels, sound systems and neon lights. Then they'd cruise the campground for hours on end like teenagers on a resort strip, playing Johnny Cash or Merle Haggard and sipping mystery beverages from red plastic cups. Naturally, this provoked a lot of golf car envy from less fortunate campers; and naturally, our predecessor had started renting golf cars at a handsome rate to satisfy this unmet demand.

When we bought the campground we had adopted a "hands-off" policy for the first year, agreeing not to change any past practices until we understood better what did or did not work, so the golf car rentals continued throughout the summer and into the fall. By late September, however, as the days were getting shorter than the nights, we realized that our rental golf cars didn't have headlights and that this posed a possible hazard. We consequently amended our rental agreement, which already required campers to have a valid driver's license and to observe the rules of the road, to stipulate that golf cars without headlights should not be operated after dark.

Then we got to Halloween.

Halloween, as anyone who has been at virtually any campground for the occasion has seen, is a time to pull out all the stops. Many campers will extensively decorate their sites, many more will parade around in the most elaborate costumes, and trick-or-treating will last for hours, as waves of costumed children and adults

*As with the distinction I've drawn between a pond and a lake, I want to note that while most people refer to those self-propelled personal vehicles as golf "carts," a cart is by definition an unpowered wagon. The more correct term is golf "car."

surge from one end of the campground to the other, oohing and ahing at the elaborate receptions awaiting them. There is a lot of candy involved for the kids, and apparently some amount of alcohol for the adults.

Alcohol was definitely at play when a costumed camper, hiding in the bushes up a short slope from one of our roads, jumped out of the darkness to scare his wife as she drove by in one of our rentals. The "plan," as we later learned, was that he was going to jump into the unoccupied passenger side of the golf car and startle the hell out of his spouse. The "reality," shaped by the combination of no headlights and alcohol-impaired judgment, was a premature leap that placed him directly and suddenly in front of the golf car as it rolled through the darkness, smashing his kneecap.

Mission accomplished: the wife was scared witless. Beyond that, the camper had medical bills north of $60,000 and filed a claim against the campground, which our insurance company—over my objections (more bad behavior rewarded!)—settled for $10,000. And after that we stopped renting golf cars, figuring they were more trouble than they were worth.

Then there's the example of David, a long-term camper who was one of the most hapless, aimless people you could imagine. When he arrived, he was so inept at towing a trailer that he clipped the corner of our office building, ripping off a gutter. The few times I managed to get a peek inside his unit I realized he was a hoarder, with paper stuffed floor to ceiling in a rig that didn't have much space in the first place. Although we emphasized to our monthlies when they first arrived that Walnut Hills was a recreational facility and not a place to put down roots, and that we expected them to have an exit strategy, David was always vague about his plans. He was going to go back to school. He would go live in Guatemala. He might take over his deceased mother's house—just as soon as he got it repaired enough to be habitable.

After two years of this aimlessness, I finally told David he had to make definite plans for the next stage of his life. Winter was coming in a few months, and because of the condition of his trailer and his own poor health, I didn't want him staying past October. He nodded and agreed that he would pull his life together.

Weeks passed. My deadline neared. One day David showed up at the office, saying he still wasn't sure what he'd be doing next, but that he'd been getting everything prepared to pull out the next day. He was having trouble with his slides, though. They were sticking, and although he'd tried poking around with a screwdriver he'd been unable to free them up— would it be possible for maintenance to come take a look? Two years of living in a trailer without ever moving—much less lubricating—the slides was definitely a problem, I thought, but David poking around anything with a screwdriver was an even bigger one.

But anything more either of us might have said was interrupted by a furious outburst on the office walkie-talkie. Smoke! Flames! A travel trailer on top of the hill was on fire— and yes, of course it was David's. Presumably sparked by his poking at a wire harness, and fueled as much by all that paper as by the flammable materials with which RV trailers are constructed, the entire rig was fully involved by the time we raced to the hilltop. When the local volunteer fire department arrived, all that awaited them was to douse the embers and ensure that the flames didn't spread to an adjacent RV.

That was the only fire we had during our tenure, but we courted a much larger conflagration one summer holiday weekend when a motor coach sprang a leak from its on-board propane tank. Although the coach itself was spotless and obviously well maintained, for some reason the propane tank was pitted with rust and suddenly began spewing its contents. The rig was immediately shut down and the volunteer fire department called, but then the confusion began: what to do? The tank couldn't be removed, and the fire department decided that moving the motorcoach was asking for trouble. I learned later that there was some discussion about evacuating the entire campground, which would have made me explode, if not the tank, but that idea was discarded as creating a logistical nightmare.

Eventually, the department decided it would simply bleed the tank dry by hooking up a hose to an auxiliary outlet and sticking the other end into a 55-gallon drum filled with water. Why having the off-gassed propane bubble up through a barrel of water made any difference was never explained to me, although the process did seem to strip out the mercaptans that give LPG its distinctive odor. But suffice to say that it took almost all night to empty the tank, the decanted propane presumably rolling into the adjacent creek and dissipating in the breeze while I huddled nearby in a lawn chair

Although tragedy was averted that time, we did have at least a couple of deaths on the property. One in particular stood out for me because it involved an elderly monthly camper living with a small dog as his only companion. Single residents were not uncommon, as men and occasionally a woman coming off a divorce would seek a temporary place to shelter while they pulled their lives together, but their isolation made them vulnerable in ways that couples and families don't experience.

In this case we were called by a camper who was worried that he hadn't seen his neighbor in several days, not even to walk his dog. The impulse toward privacy is so strong on a campground that he had been reluctant to go banging on the neighbor's door, but would we check up on him? I rode up and knocked on the locked trailer, provoking a lot of barking but no other response. Closed venetian blinds kept me from seeing in, but a light was on in the bedroom and I could hear a television. The camper's car was in its normal parking spot.

I called the missing camper's son, who lived in another state, and was told he hadn't heard from his father in several days and that his calls had gone unanswered. At that point I finally called the sheriff's department, and while the responding deputies reluctantly agreed that the circumstances pointed to only one conclusion, there was no mistaking what awaited them when they pried open the trailer door and got a whiff. Whether the camper's heart attack could have been treated if someone had been on hand to call for immediate medical assistance is unknowable, but I realized there were several other seasonal campers whom I wouldn't see for weeks on end, underscoring the fragility of their lives.

(One resource we added to the campground shortly after we bought it was the purchase of two defibrillators, one mounted in the office and one on the outside wall of the upper bathhouse, less than a hundred feet from the seasonal sites. In this case it was irrelevant, but I've long wondered why such devices aren't as common at campgrounds as they are in most hotels and motels—especially since a significant segment of the camping public has reached heart-attack age.)

Death and destruction may follow us all, but some of the more profound problems we encountered were dragged into our midst by the campers themselves, when they could as easily have left them at home. None was more nettlesome than the human impulse to flaunt one's beliefs, thrusting them into other people's faces as a declaration of one's identity and allegiances without regard for what response that might evoke, or what hurt it might cause.

Bumper stickers I could live with; ditto for T-shirts, despite the deliberately provocative messages on them that have become more commonplace. But it was the flags that prompted the most dissension and discussion within our family, streaming from the back bumpers of pick-up trucks, planted on poles in front of parked RVs, flapping from antennas rising ten or 20 feet above RV roofs. American flags, Confederate flags, Marine Corps banners, Trump flags of every description—the RVing public, if you were judging only by the flag array, consisted largely of gun-toting, Bible-thumping Dixiecrats and right-wing militants. And, hell, we *were* in rural mountain Virginia.

But we also knew that many—perhaps even most—of our campers were nothing like that. We had a growing number of gay and lesbian couples who had found us hospitable, and we were seeing a small but growing number of black, brown and

Asian campers who were dipping their toes into formerly all-white campground waters. More young and often clearly liberal campers from northern Virginia and the D.C. and Richmond metro areas were discovering us. All these people, as a rule, were not flag-waving types, so there had to be an element of surprise, if not apprehension for some, when they found themselves amidst so many symbols of intolerance.

Offensive as much of this was, I'm also a passionate believer in free speech and have long embraced the idea that more speech, not less, is the best antidote to ignorance. Carin or my younger daughter, Erika, would ask me why we didn't simply ban the most offensive flags, and I would respond by asking them where they would draw the line—and how they would explain the ban to some campers while permitting others to fly less objectionable flags without challenge. Well, they would answer, let's just ban *all* flags, which had a certain attractive simplicity, until I asked if that prohibition would extend to the American flag as well. On the Fourth of July. Or Memorial Day.

There was no easy answer, so the uneasy status quo prevailed—for the most part.

One exception occurred in 2017, when we employed two German students for the season through the federal J-1 visa program. That was the summer of brown-shirted neo-fascists marching in nearby Charlottesville to protest the planned removal of a statue of Robert E. Lee, a demonstration that deeply shook both of our guest workers because of the disturbing parallels they saw with their own country's history. Why, they wanted to know, were Americans still flying the Confederate flag more than 100 years after the defeat of that failed insurrection? More to the point, they demanded, why were we allowing the flag on our property?

That led to long, sometimes passionate conversations about free speech and the struggle of ideas, culminating in their request to be allowed to also fly flags—of their choosing. Of course, I replied.

As it happened, the two students shared a campground-owned travel trailer next to a monthly site occupied by an ex-Marine and his wife who had been returning to Walnut Hills each summer for more than a decade, even after they moved to Florida. Each summer they would erect several flags at the front edge of their site, including the Stars and Bars. This summer, however, they woke up one day to neighbors flying a "Black Lives Matter" flag, followed soon thereafter by an LGBTQ rainbow banner. After that, the ex-Marine spent his summers elsewhere.

As time passed, however, the flag-waving became more shrill, propelled by the ever-increasing zealousness of Trump supporters. I finally drew the line when a new monthly guest put up a banner that must have been eight feet long, depicting Trump as a bazooka-wielding Rambo and the message "No more bullshit." On one level I admired the unconscious parody of idolizing a draft-dodger as the ultimate icon of militant hyper-masculinity while declaiming against "bullshit," but at the same time I doubted that everyone would experience the same inner chuckle I did—indeed, that some of our campers might become understandably enraged at this in-your-face provocation.

So I made him take it down. He argued, saying he had a right to free speech, and I agreed that he did—in a public space. If he wanted to stand on a street corner, fly his flag and run his mouth, no problem, but this was my property, not his. And just to cap it off, although my personal language often runs in a direction sometimes described as "salty," this was a family campground and I had a problem with flaunting the word "bullshit" for all to see. At the end of the month he, too, took his business elsewhere, which was just fine by me.

The darker side of human nature found still other ways of intruding, however, notwithstanding all our efforts to make Walnut Hills a haven from the outside world. One of the most unexpected came in a phone call from the campground's former owner, who asked if I knew that one of the men on the state's "Sex Offender and Crimes Against Minors Registry," operated by the Virginia State Police, had given the campground as his home address. I did not—didn't even know that it was possible to get emailed updates about the registry on a regular basis. Worse yet, we couldn't find anyone by that name in our records. After some sleuthing, however, we learned that the sex offender was a friend of a couple that was renting one of our long-term sites and that he had moved in with them without telling us, which in itself violated our rules.

We ended up evicting all three campers, ousting the couple for violating their terms of stay. But the episode did not end quietly, as the sex offender's mother stormed into our registration office and loudly demanded to know why we were kicking out her grown son—something that should have been obvious even to the most doting parent—as a line of campers waited to check in, some with children in tow. After that we had two similar instances, of older men who at different times rented monthly sites before we learned of their place on the registry, and in truth I felt bad about kicking them out. Both men had led quiet and solitary lives while with us, and when I told them they would have to leave, responded with sad resignation. But after the second time the message got out, and Walnut Hills did not pop up on any subsequent registry updates.

Just like a hotel suite, but with wooden walls.

6. One big, happy family

BUYING WALNUT HILLS meant more than just buying a campground—it was more like a marriage, and a marriage to someone with 500 other brides at that.

The Staunton/Walnut Hills KOA, as it was known, had already been a KOA for three years when we stepped in. But because each KOA franchise agreement runs five years, the seller required us to renew the franchise so he wouldn't be liable for two years of prorated franchise fees. That also meant that Kampgrounds of America had to approve us as buyers, even though it had no ownership stake in the campground itself, an unanticipated complication that nevertheless proved of little consequence—then.

But as with any marriage, we should have put a lot more thought and research into this new family we were joining. We knew nothing about the company or what demands it would place on us, and nothing about the relationship it had with its franchised operators or how they viewed their experience. On the other hand, we knew that it was a major presence in the campground industry, and both KOA and the Jellystone system had been strongly promoted by Darrell Hess, our broker, as demonstrably super-charging reservations and income for campgrounds that made the switch. Best of all, buying an existing KOA meant we would avoid the $35,000 upfront cost of becoming a new franchise down the road, should we decide that's what we wanted.

Financial considerations aside, there was the very real comfort of knowing that as a KOA we would not be alone in this venture—that an experienced organization would have our backs. We may have done a decent amount of RVing ourselves, but that history no more prepared us for running a campground than eating a steak prepared us to become ranchers. A frank appraisal would conclude that we knew absolutely nothing about a business to which we were committing every bit of our time and money, and that has got to be the very definition of scary.

It therefore was with a great sense of relief that daughter Erika and I got on a plane in February 2013 to fly to KOA headquarters in Billings, Montana, just days after our closing. We were about to attend "KOA University," a week-long training session that KOA requires all new franchisees to attend so they can learn its reservation system, its corporate history and culture, and the resources a network of 500 or so campgrounds could provide our little operation.

(This last point was emphasized by KOA itself a few years later, when it ran a series of full-page ads in a leading trade publication under the headline, "What could *you* do with **an extra $35,600?**" [emphases in the original]. That's how much the ad calculated was the worth of services received by KOA franchisees from "an entire team of one-of-a-kind Marketing and Operational experts," including a professional website, the online reservation system, national directory listings, remodeling and site design services, and on and on. We later calculated that this valuation was inflated by nearly 100%.)

Unfortunately, the KOA training session was the high point of our relationship.

At least half of our time in Billings was devoted to learning how to navigate KampSight, a creaky, DOS-based reservations software system that even then was eating the dust of the point-and-click systems used by hotels and motels. While other campgrounds were already adopting versions of those systems specifically adapted for the camping industry, like Campspot and Campground Manager, KOA had decided it would develop its own software, dubbed "K2," and until then the franchisees would have to muddle along with KampSight. Unfortunately, the company that should have been a leading innovator in this area repeatedly fumbled the ball, producing so many buggy versions of K2 that it didn't get all its franchisees on the same page until early 2021.*

When not staring at power-point presentations, we were given a tour of the building and introduced to headquarters personnel, shown various artifacts and historical photos tracing KOA's evolution since 1962, and shown the variety of KOA-branded merchandize we could order for our campground stores. There was a lot of branded merchandise. We also learned that the 'K' in 'KOA' was adopted because it enhances KOA's trademarked tepee-style logo,** that KOA is actually owned by a single businessman, Oscar Tang, and that at one time there were nearly 900 KOAs, including some in Mexico and Japan. Toward the end of our week we also had one-on-one meetings with staff members who asked us what specific problems they could help us address—a pointless invitation at the time, given that we'd been campground owners for less than a week and still didn't know what we didn't know. Unfortu-

---

*Fun fact, suggesting that identity is destiny so be careful when naming things: the original K2, on the Chinese-Pakistani border in the Karakorum Range, has killed 87 climbers since 1954—more, percentage-wise, than Mount Everest.

**Or at least that's the corporate mythology. An alternate explanation is that the nascent company tried to trademark "Campgrounds of America" but was denied because "campground" was a common word. Both versions may be true.

nately, that invitation was never renewed.

Woven throughout all these interactions was a relentless, cheery effort to portray KOA and its franchisees as one big family, with the parent company helping the franchisees and the franchisees reciprocating in turn, a virtuous circle of camaraderie and pioneer helpfulness. That same upbeat vibe pervaded the company's annual conventions, all of which we attended and all of which invariably featured rosy reports on the previous year and even brighter forecasts for the future, as well as pumped-up motivational speakers to get our juices flowing, raffles, live music and a whole lot of corporate yellow. But the reality was that after we returned from Billings, we didn't see or hear from anyone at KOA for months, even as we began to feel its heavy corporate hand.

One issue we encountered almost immediately was our disagreement with the way KOA administered the so-called "marshmallow reviews," since supplanted by a more conventional one-to-five stars rating system that appears at the top of every KOA campground landing page—the "home" page for each campground, but one over which those campgrounds have no control. Although KOA initially told franchisees they would be able to remove up to 2% of reviews posted by "unreasonable" campers, the company soon back-pedaled out of a belated concern that it was courting a public relations nightmare—that the camping public would become furious if it began to view such content policing as censorship.

That might have been a convincing, if arguable,* rationale had it been universally applied. But KOA also recognized that it couldn't leave the floodgates wide open—that there inevitably would be some campers who would write mean and hurtful (even untruthful!) things that would reflect badly on the company itself. So while we were not allowed to protect ourselves from malicious

---

*Indeed, years of increasingly abusive and mendacious commentary have convinced many social media sites to oversee more actively what they're publishing. Moreover, it bears repeating that "censorship" applies to government action, not to private interests.

or deceitful attacks on our image and reputation, KOA reserved the right to do so on our—and its own—behalf. As one KOA executive acknowledged to us, "On a rare occasion we remove a customer comment because of the use of profanity, abusive language or personal attack on an owner or manager." How nice. And how paternal.

That was our first clue that our business needs would always come second to the corporate parent's, an asymmetric relationship to which we had committed all our resources but in which we were regarded as just one of 500 more or less interchangeable cogs. In the years that followed, we would learn repeatedly that while our concerns or ideas might be received politely (and they usually were) and might even result in some minor tweaking of the latest corporate initiative, once a direction was set there would be few course corrections.

We were hardly the only franchisee complaining about KOA's management of camper reviews, and we also were not alone in resisting its "brand positioning" initiative, which kicked off just as we came into the system. This was the company's decision to segment its portfolio into three groupings, designated as "Journey," "Holiday" and "Resort," each with its own minimum standards targeting a different segment of the camping public. The rationale was that such branding distinctions would give the public a better idea of what services and facilities to expect at each campground; the reaction among many KOA franchisees, on the other hand, was that such segmentation would create a "good, better, best" ranking within a system that was still having trouble enforcing just one across-the-board set of standards.*

For us, a bigger issue was that roughly one-third of our campers fit into the "Journey" category, of travelers looking for an overnight stay, while two-thirds belonged in the "Holiday" cate-

---

*Our suggestion—complete with artwork—that KOA create a fourth, "Classic" category for those of us stuck in the past was ignored. If Coca-Cola had been as stubborn, more Americans would be drinking Pepsi today.

gory of campers staying for several nights of outdoor recreation. Why would we run the risk of advertising ourselves as one kind of campground or another and possibly chase away business that didn't fit within an arbitrary definition? Yet this initiative, as was true of the marshmallow reviews, remained impervious to grass-roots complaints, and with each passing year the franchisees experienced growing pressure to declare themselves in one camp (pun intended) or another. By the end of 2020, all had.

Both those examples underscored the inescapable tension between a national franchise with a top-down decision-making process trying to establish a uniform set of standards, and a far-flung assortment of independently owned campgrounds whose owners might have other ideas. Nor was there unanimity among the owners themselves, many of whom couldn't be bothered to wade in the weeds on various policy issues, and many others who embraced just about anything KOA proposed: this was the market leader, after all, so how wrong could it be? And for campgrounds that had come into the system and seen their annual revenues pop 10% to 20% in the first year, thanks to the KOA marketing juggernaut, sticking with the leader was a no-brainer.

For us and others, however, the inescapable fact was that this was *our* campground, not KOA's. While much of the camping public thinks all KOAs have a single corporate owner, all but a score or so of the KOAs are individually owned (or, increasingly, owned by non-KOA companies) in which KOA has no ownership stake whatsoever. Any of those franchisees can leave the system without penalty after the franchise period expires, and many do, which is why the number of KOAs has been increasing at only a modest rate. As we would remind ourselves, it was *our* money at stake, *our* sweat that kept things humming and *our* relationships with our campers that kept them coming back.

Moreover, as one corporate initiative or dictate after another spewed forth from Billings, it became ever more clear to us that KOA's identity was shaped not by boots-on-the-ground campground owners but by a PR and marketing brain-trust with little if any first-hand campground management experience. No surprise, really, that a building full of marketing and PR types, accountants, and software developers—virtually none of whom had ever owned or operated a campground—would spend their working hours pushing gift cards, loading up the Value Kard program with little wanted "partner benefits," hyping dynamic pricing models and advocating for the transformation of campgrounds into open-air living rooms, with patio furniture and "fire experiences." Having thus demonstrated their lack of understanding of the challenges we faced, almost the entire brain trust would then empty out and go home on the weekends and holidays—which is to say, at times of peak camping demand, when critical problems at the franchisees were most likely to emerge.[*]

Indeed, while KOA was founded—as was impressed on us at KOA University—to meet the needs of campers traveling the northern tier to reach the World's Fair in Seattle, over time the company has drifted ever more steadily away from its tenting and RVing roots. To a significant extent, this drift can be traced to the turn of the century, when Jim Rogers became the company's president and chief executive officer after 22 years as an executive at Harrah's Enterprises, a hotel and casino operator. Stepping into the top KOA position in 2000, he brought with him a conviction that commercial campgrounds were simply a lodging industry that had failed to keep up with the times. As he told Forbes magazine in a 2012 interview, "the casino business is so cutting edge and the camping industry is so 'back of the woods'" that he was having a lot of fun applying "a few things I learned in the casino hotel business" to KOA.

"KOA is really all about making outdoor adventure easy," Rogers added, before gushing over the company's enthusiastic em-

---

[*]Another example of the disconnect between KOA and its franchisees was personified by its 2017 hiring of Darin Uselman as its chief contact person with the franchisees. Uselman, who had never owned or operated a campground, had been making his living as a professional golfer. At this writing, he's KOA's chief operating officer.

brace of deluxe cabins. "They are just like a suite in a hotel except the interior is all wood," he explained, projecting that this would be the system's biggest growth area over the next three to five years.

Over his 15 years as chief executive, Rogers hugely reshaped KOA's culture and practices to more closely resemble the industry that had molded his own perspective. The Value Kard program, for example, was modeled on casino "player cards," which are distributed to repeat gamblers as a way of keeping track of the best customers and rewarding them accordingly. "We learned the customer was what we called the 'recognition driven gambler," he told Forbes. "The same is true in most hospitality experiences." He also was largely responsible for introducing a new vocabulary that now permeates KOA, with its emphasis on the "customer experience," "transcendent hospitality" and "wow factors."

But it was Rogers' emphasis on deluxe cabins that filtered down most aggressively to the franchisee level, since it was going to be up to the individual campground owners to actually invest in such amenities—KOA wasn't going to buy them. So from the start we were awash in KOA propaganda about deluxe cabins being the next big thing in camping, with KOA promising to forsake royalties on new units in the first year and its financing partner, Independence Bank, promoting a "go with the flow" financing plan that would eliminate loan repayments in the off-season. By 2016 the overall KOA inventory of deluxe cabins was nearing 3,000, or double the number in the four years since Rogers had talked to Forbes.

Whether the camping public really wanted more cabins was not addressed in any meaningful fashion, nor did the company analyze whether the money spent on cabins would have been better expended on increasing the number of available RV sites—which in hindsight, given the recent explosion in demand for RV sites, looks like a no-brainer. Instead, the company simplistically promoted the cabins because they've "proven themselves to be moneymakers for KOA owners." The math it used to justify that claim? That, on average, a deluxe cabin pulled in more than

$11,000 in 2015, or just under $125 per camper night—a jolly number indeed, especially when compared with the average revenue generated by an RV site.

But *taking* money is not the same as *making* money, and cabins are a pricey investment. Base prices at that time for the Cavco models that KOA favored ran around $30,000 and up, to which a campground owner had to add shipping costs, site preparation, set-up and skirting expenses and all the "interior décor," to use KOA's phrase: furniture, dishes, cookware, appliances, a flat-panel TV. Factor in the additional cost of linens, laundry, cleaning staff and supplies—all things RVers provide for themselves—as well as maintenance upkeep and replacement of trashed or stolen furnishings, and annual gross revenues of $11,000 per cabin suddenly looked much less enticing. Meanwhile, our patio RV sites—regular RV sites that cost around $5,000 to up-grade with a concrete deck, patio furniture, a raised fire ring and a gas grill—were each grossing an average of $10,435 that same year.

Aside from the dubious economics of plunging into a rustic version of a Motel 6, KOA's push into cabins signaled for us a loss of focus on the company's core activity: "back of the woods" camping, in Rogers' dismissive phrase. Ever reliant on poll-taking to determine what its customer base is seeking—a strong clue that a company has lost its way—KOA nevertheless disregarded or misinterpreted input like its own 2015 questionnaire, in which 55% of respondents, when asked their "key reasons for camping," responded that "camping allows me to reconnect with nature and the outdoors." Instead, the highlighted preference was for responses like the quote in the 2014 annual report, attributed to a KOA camper, that declared: "Of all the camping I've done in my life, none has ever included air conditioning or a flat screen TV with cable! With new Deluxe Cabins, KOA is really taking camping to a whole new level."

Indeed.

Following close on the heels of the cabin campaign was KOA's embrace of "glamping," a portmanteau of "glamorous" and "camping" that a cynic might construe as meaning neither. Safari tents, eco-pods, yurts, tree houses, tepees, covered "wagons"—all were swept into glamping's big tent. At its extreme, KOA in 2020 took this emphasis to its logical conclusion by eliminating all 100 RV spaces at a campground in Maine and replacing them with large safari tents on wooden platforms, each with its own bathroom with hot and cold running water. With the focus thus shifted to lodging as an end in itself, rather than as a way of experiencing an environment that might otherwise be inaccessible or intolerable, there's no surprise that KOA's attention increasingly has turned away from nature and toward comfort.

The apotheosis of this trend was reached in 2019, when the company unveiled its "Campground of the Future" animated project. The interactive on-line display, replete with automated check-ins and firewood-delivering robots, had its priorities signaled in a company press release that opened with the explanation that the Campground of the Future "includes expanded technology offerings." Its five different "environments" included "camping" on manmade ocean causeways and in underwater glass bubbles, as well as on urban rooftops, and the project overall seemed to be greeted by the campground industry with a lot of gee-whiz wonder and only a soupcon of skepticism. Even the few critics seemed content to fall back on the "well, at least it's a starting point for discussion" trope, apparently without comprehending that the conversation increasingly was being steered away from the natural world.

But while KOA dreamed its big dreams, the only corporate representatives we saw were our annual inspection team and, twice in our first year, our "business development rep," who spent his time teaching me how better to integrate our KampSite reservations system with our QuickBooks accounting platform. While that was helpful and appreciated, I couldn't understand why KOA wasn't taking a more active interest in what we were doing—why the "business development" rep wasn't helping us develop the business. When I finally got around to asking him, at one of KOA's annual conventions after not seeing him for several years, his bland response was, "Oh, it looked to us like you know what you're do-ing."

That was reassuring—sort of—and to a significant extent supported by the numbers, but it did raise the question of why, then, we needed KOA in the first place. Our revenues were increasing nicely, year over year. Our marshmallow review scores eventually reached the top 20% of the system, and our annual inspection reports to determine if we met KOA's standards were consistently stellar, even as I resolutely ignored their edicts about such minutiae as how many hooks we should have in the shower stalls or what kind of latch we should install on our dog-park gates. And after 2013, when we received the President's Award, we won the more prestigious Founder's Award—presented to the franchisees with the highest overall rankings—four years running.

Then again, the awards reminded me of Lake Woebegone, where every child was above average: with more than half of all KOAs getting the Founders Award, what was the distinction that KOA was recognizing? What, indeed, were we getting from KOA that was worthwhile? Put another way, if we knew what we were doing, why did we need KOA?

The one thing I did know was that KOA was getting a lot of money from us: 10% of all our site revenues, plus an annual franchise administrative fee. And I knew we were leaving money on the table each year, in the form of KOA's Value Kard discounts and revenue lost to Value Kard "appreciation" events, which translated into free camping nights. Put it all together and our annual "KOA tax" grew to $70,000 by 2017, of which $60,000 was in direct payments to the company. Meanwhile, the dollar value of our KOA-related registrations kept dropping as a percentage of our registration income, to just 16% that same year, while the absolute number of KOA campers was in a slower decline.

In short, the more we grew the more we contributed to KOA's coffers, even though we weren't getting any more value from the company from one year to the next. Indeed, it was worse than that, because a significant chunk of the money KOA got from its franchisees was spent on buying and improving corporate-owned RV campgrounds. Rather than thinking about ways to use that income to pull up the system's underperformers—and there always have been a fair number of those, hobbled by undercapitalization and a downward spiral of stagnant or declining revenues fed by poor reviews—KOA was in effect competing with the rest of us. And we were its bankers.

Adding insult to injury, I realized that the money we were sending to KOA was financing all those glitzy but dubious initiatives like the Campground of the Future. Our success was only encouraging the idiots. Something had to change.

Under the maples on top of the hill.

7. Spitting out the yellow Kool Aid

WHEN OUR DAUGHTERS and their husbands said they wanted to join us in our campground venture, Carin and I insisted on just one condition: each of the couples had to make an initial five-year commitment. If we were going to take on an investment big enough to support all of us, we weren't going to get in neck-deep only to have someone say, a year or two later, that it was too much work or that they had something else they'd rather be doing. Five years seemed like more than a whim but less than a lifetime. It also happened to be the length of a KOA franchise contract.

So as we entered the final months of 2017, we had two issues to discuss: was everyone willing to re-up for another five years—and if so, would it be as a KOA? Or would we try to go it alone? If we were going to continue, in any capacity, the decision would have to be unanimous: like a three-legged stool, we would not be able to stand with one support missing. I needed Mitch to run the maintenance end of things because it was a bigger job than I could handle; ditto for Erika managing the store and office.

Neither of them had the skills or experience to take on the other's responsibilities, and both needed me to run the business overall. (As I would respond when someone would ask me what my job was, "I make it possible for everyone else to do their jobs.")

Always the over-thinker, I headed into our family meeting with a three-page analysis intended to kick off the discussion. I could have spared myself the effort. Although my number-crunching made a persuasive—but not definitive—case for leaving the franchise, everyone else had already decided that we didn't need or want to continue as a KOA franchise. Enough with the yellow shirts! On the other hand, the family agreed, we did want to stay in the campground business for another five- year hitch.

But while we were contemplating our future, so was KOA. Months before our franchise was to expire, we started getting informal inquiries about our intentions, followed around the time of our family meeting by a formal franchise renewal letter evoking the "one big family" myth by thanking us for choosing "to partner" with KOA. What that really meant, notwithstanding language in the agreement stipulating that it had been "negotiated" by both parties, was an expectation that we would sign off on several thousand words of new or deleted language without modification. Take it or leave it, partner.[*]

Interestingly, the new language made explicit the heavy-handedness we had already experienced informally. Page after page of the agreement had already outlined a franchisee's obligations to KOA, while KOA's reciprocal duties were limited to just four sentences. But just to make sure everyone understood who was calling the shots, KOA had inserted a brand-new section asserting its exclusive right to exercise its business judgment "without regard to its effect on any individual franchisee or park/campground."

---

[*]This self-delusional theme was repeated in a company-wide Christmas letter a few weeks later from then-chief executive Pat Hittmeier, in which he commented on how business leaders in other industries simply "don't understand" the "partnership bond" that exists between KOA and its franchisees. Us, neither.

Moreover, "KOA's judgment shall prevail even in cases where other alternatives may be reasonable"— which, in our view, was hardly reasonable at all. This was a "partnership"?

KOA soon also made it abundantly clear, first in email exchanges and then in one particularly strained face-to-face meeting, that its claim about negotiations was not to be taken seriously and that it wasn't about to change any of the prerogatives it had carved out for itself. Nor was it willing to modify its fee structure, even though Jellystone, for example, has a tiered system that reduces its cut of a franchisee's revenues as they hit certain growth benchmarks. And while KOA's new franchise agreement included the claim that "there are times when we will look at an individual campground's situation and negotiate modifications" to the standard franchise fees, our renewal apparently was not going to be one of those times.

The combination of high fees and high-handedness, coming on top of KOA's five-year neglect of our interests and its increasingly disconnected corporate culture, finally convinced me— our family's last hold-out—to pull the plug. On January 8, 2018, I wrote to KOA announcing our decision not to renew. We would go it alone—but then, we pretty much already had been.

While I shared the rest of my family's irritation at KOA, my reluctance to jump for the exits was rooted in the financial analysis that everyone else was preferring not to dwell on. We all knew that we were pumping a lot of money into Billings—more than a quarter of a million dollars to that date. But some of that money was paying for services we would have to replace, notably a reservation system, a credit card processor and advertising. We also were going to have to pay numerous conversion costs, including new interstate highway signs and new entrance and office signs, as well as new stationery, business cards, rack cards, guest guides and employee t-shirts. Anything with a KOA logo, including all branded store merchandise, would have to be modified or discarded.

But the big unknown was how much business we would lose. How many of our campers, wedded to their KOA Value

Kards, would switch their business to another KOA once we were no longer honoring their discount? How many campers would we lose because of sheer brand loyalty, notably among the many Canadians who unabashedly love their "koas" (typically pronounced by them as a single word rhyming with "boas," rather than as an acronym)? Because KOA card-carrying members had been a declining percentage of our growing customer base, it appeared to me that if we retained just 25% of our KOA business we would be even—that the loss of 75% of our KOA customers would be offset by our savings from retained franchise fees. A mere 50% retention rate would cover my estimated cost of the services we would now be funding ourselves—and anything more than that was gravy.

But I didn't know what the actual attrition rate would be, and not knowing was scary.

Now, having notified KOA of our decision, we had to scramble. We had just three weeks to design a new logo, order and install new signs and sign up with a new reservation system and credit card processor. Having decided to become a Good Sam affiliate* because of the marketing exposure this would bring, we bought several thousand dollars in advertising and printed round stickers with Good Sam logos that we could slap over the KOA logo on the campground's many internal signs. We held a fire sale of all KOA-branded merchandise in our store, bought new red employee t-shirts to replace KOA's yellow, changed our voice-mail messages and redid the website that we had maintained—thankfully! —in parallel with the home page KOA provided.

Mostly, everything was done within the allotted time, although getting the highway department to replace the KOA logo on its interstate signs with a Good Sam one took a bit longer. But in mid-February, as we started breathing more easily, KOA threw us another curve ball: an email sent to everyone on our extensive

---

*While KOA and Jellystone are franchisees, Good Sam is an affiliate program that any campground can join for less than $1,000 a year in purchased advertising. Affiliates do not pay royalty fees and can renew on an annual basis.

email list, trumpeting "Experience great KOAs!" The message continued, "Because we know you love KOA, we wanted to let you know that the Staunton/Walnut Hills location in Virginia is no longer a KOA Campground. But, we have great news! There are a lot of other wonderful KOAs in that area."

The wording, without context or additional explanation, was just ambiguous enough to get the phone ringing with a flurry of anxious callers wanting to know if we had gone out of business. KOA members who had booked sites for the coming season were wondering if we were going to honor their reservations—or their KOA discounts (yes, and yes). And if they wanted to cancel their reservations, would they get their deposits back from us or from KOA corporate, and how would that happen?

Seething over KOA's nonchalant misdirection, I fired off an irate email to Pat Hittmeier that detailed the effect of his company's email on our—and his! —customers and requested a public clarification. We had made every effort "to terminate our relationship with KOA in a professional and respectful way," I wrote, before adding: "Whether intentionally or carelessly, you have taken the low road—but that only reinforces my contention that KOA is generally oblivious to how its actions affect the franchisees."

Hittmeier's response, in trademark "father knows best" mode, inadvertently made my point by denying that KOA had created a problem. "We reviewed the email and although I see how it might be misinterpreted, we don't believe it merits a retraction," he wrote, placing the onus on those who received KOA's email rather than on those who wrote it. Moreover, he added, in an especially gratuitous suggestion, KOA had created a great marketing entree for us: "I would suggest and I am not being flippant, that you might want to take this opportunity and email all your data base and get them excited about visiting you this year." What a swell idea!

(In subsequent years, I learned that our experience had not been that unusual—and, indeed, that we may have gotten off relatively lightly. For example, when the KOA in Terre Haute dropped its franchise but continued as an independent campground, anyone Googling its name would have been taken to a page showing a picture of the campground, a location map, and the very bold words, "Permanently Closed." For former KOA campgrounds that hadn't maintained a separate web site, that was tantamount to a death sentence.)

Wisely or otherwise, we did not go quietly into the night, and the feedback was fascinating. Following a column I wrote about our decision for RVTravel, an independent and respected online presence that targets the RVing community, I was taken aback by the amount and intensity of anti-KOA feeling among many campers. I heard from campers who complained that KOA campgrounds are too expensive and layer on too many additional fees, meriting the "Keep On Adding" label. Campers who complained that KOA campgrounds are too crowded and cramped, with too many sites shoe-horned into too small an area. Campers who waxed vitriolic about KOA campgrounds that are inadequately maintained or KOA employees who are surly or campgrounds that are too close to a highway or railroad tracks or airport runways. . . .

There was such an avalanche of negativity that I became uncomfortable with the sweeping generalizations sent our way by campers trying to be supportive. At the same time, clearly there was a groundswell of anti-KOA feeling to which I, as a KOA owner, had never been exposed. I wondered if KOA's marketing machine would ever have the nerve to tap into it and perhaps learn something useful.

In the months that followed, I also heard from several people who were building or buying a campground and were thinking about seeking a KOA franchise. Understandably, they wanted to know why we would jump a ship that they were thinking of boarding. I would relate our experience and conclude that unless they thought joining KOA would actually boost business long-term— for example, if they were in a remote location not readily accessible to major highways or tourist attractions and needed KOA's marketing muscle—I didn't foresee a reasonable return on the money they'd be spending. Almost invariably, however, it wasn't the money that was foremost in their thoughts: it was the desire for a safety net.

A similar anxiety came through from the handful of existing KOA franchisees who contacted me because they also were thinking of leaving, but who were worried about their odds of making it on their own. For me, that was the most insidious aspect of being in a system that fosters learned helplessness.

To be sure, that first year of going it alone was not easy. While I had calculated we'd be holding our own if we didn't lose more than $40,000 to $45,000 in revenues, total income for 2018 plunged $65,000. On closer examination, however, I became convinced that what had really hurt us was the weather. An exceptionally wet autumn, including double the normal rainfall for September, had forced us to close a part of the campground just ahead of the historically busy month of October. Advance reservations also took a hit, and the year trailed off dismally. Still, we had no choice but to keep going—and so it was with a huge sense of relief that we saw the pendulum swing back in 2019. With a return to more normal precipitation patterns and a hot summer, camper nights and our income rebounded to the levels we'd seen our last year as a KOA—but without KOA's costs.

Now we truly were captains of our fate. Or so we thought, until the pandemic hit us like a ton of bricks.

Dredging the lake, a major undertaking.

8. It takes a village

EXCEPT FOR THE VERY SMALLEST campgrounds, anyone who
wants to operate a facility that will be hosting thousands of visitors a year is going to need help. And as we soon learned, that is
no easy need to fill.

The operating premise behind a small campground is that
the owner-operators will provide all or most of the labor, perhaps
drawing a nominal wage but reinvesting as much as possible to
improve the property, and thus through sweat equity build value
that can be realized when the campground is sold. In this model,
additional labor becomes an expense rather than an asset; it sub-
tracts from available reinvestment capital, and so must be controlled as rigorously as possible. Anything a campground owner
(or his family) can do for himself, he will: mow the grass, cut and
split firewood, launder campground linens, perform routine tool
and vehicle maintenance.

But as the amount of work grows to exceed an owning
family's available time or energy, employees must be hired—and

that's where things get tricky. A large campground can afford to view at least some employees as investments, as essential as a good tractor or computer system for its efficient operation, and therefore worthy of the kind of pay and benefits needed to attract and retain good workers. At some point it also can afford to farm out some work, such as buying bundled firewood from a vendor instead of splitting its own, or using a commercial laundry, or even hiring a lawn-care company to take care of the grounds. But a campground small enough for sweat equity to be a significant factor in value creation can't afford all that.

That's where we were. When Carin and I bought Walnut Hills, we were fortunate in that we were both receiving Social Security payments and so could get by without a paycheck. But while one of our sons-in-law headed up the maintenance staff, and one of our daughters ran the store and office, we still had to pay them enough to live on and had to hire additional employees as well. Quite a few additional employees, it turned out: with a front office and store open 86 hours a week and at least two desk clerks needed at all times to handle the phones and counter—three when things got busy—we needed a minimum of six office staff. A dozen cabins and two bathhouses, plus the game room and pavilion, required at least two housekeepers to keep everything clean—and three would have been better. And 15 to 20 acres of lawn to mow and edge, 126 RV sites to clean and keep trim, a mile-and-a-half of internal gravel roads to scrape and level, a honey wagon to operate and all the maintenance issues created by all our buildings and infrastructure, meant we needed at least four additional maintenance or groundskeeping workers.

In short, we had to find 12 to 15 employees each year. We had to find employees who were willing to work for little more than minimum wage, because that's all we could afford. And we had to find employees who would know from day one that they'd be without a job by November, when the season would end and we'd need no more than one or two people to help us get through the winter. Where do you find people like that?

We created the most attractive working conditions we could within our limited means, trying to make the workplace as flexible and accommodating of our employees' needs as we could. Although we couldn't afford a workplace health insurance plan, we paid up to $350 a month toward their premiums for employees who enrolled in the Affordable Care Act. We provided free work gloves and ear and eye protection to our maintenance workers and paid up to $100 a year toward the cost of new work boots. We held an annual Christmas dinner, at which we distributed bonus checks.

Still, there was no getting around the fact that there were better paying and more stable job opportunities all around us, and the job applicants who found us were usually just scraping by, for one reason or another. People who had choices would go to work at one of the local manufacturing plants, like Hershey or Hollister, which not only paid better but offered full-time employment year-round. Or they'd go to work at a local fast-food restaurant, where the pay was no better but the job wouldn't end in six months. The applicants we ended up seeing were disproportionately people who had fallen on hard times and gotten knocked down every time they started pulling themselves back up.

An astonishing percentage of our applicants, for example, were driving on a suspended driver's license. Quite often this was because of a DWI citation, but until the law was changed in July 2019, a Virginia driver's license also could be suspended over unpaid fines or court costs for offenses completely unrelated to driving. The offenders would continue driving on their suspended licenses anyway, because that's the only way they could get around in a rural community, so of course the financial hole they'd dug would only get deeper the next time they got nailed, which they almost invariably were.

Indeed, nothing in our research and study for running a business had prepared me for the court-ordered liens and garnishments that arrived in our mail with remorseless regularity. I ended up keeping notes in a file I would dig out each payday to see which employee I would have to dock that week and for how much, and often it would be more than one employee per pay period. At least the court costs or fines would get paid off within a set period. Garnishment of child-support payments, on the other hand, presumably would continue throughout an employee's tenure, and I was shocked to learn that such dunning could take a bite of up to 65% of wages, regardless of any other unrelated garnishments and without any acknowledgment of changes in working hours or how much an employee might be left to live on.

Child support payments sound like a sacrosanct obligation, and the case workers assigned by the state to gather that money can sound downright sanctimonious in its pursuit. But things look quite a bit different when your garnished employee's spouse is in prison, her children are being taken care of by other relatives and the employee herself has severe medical and cognitive issues, not to mention a felony record for physical assault. You can't squeeze blood from a stone, but the state tried—and not long after it reduced her income to less than $90 a week, the employee in this example quit. She wasn't *that* cognitively impaired.

Hiring from the bottom of the local labor pool meant a revolving door of employees, with some coming back a second or even a third time before we finally said "enough." Some quit in anger over perceived slights, claiming they'd been "disrespected," which usually meant they took issue with having their work performance evaluated; some just stopped showing up for work, without any explanation. Some got better jobs, which we couldn't fault, and some got fired, like the housekeeper whose theft of housekeeping supplies might have gone unnoticed had she not decided to also start stealing gasoline. And some, fortunately, kept plugging away over the years, justifying our faith in overlooking their prison stints or repeated medical emergencies.

One alternative labor supply that many campgrounds turn to is work campers (sometimes also written as workampers). Usually full-time Rvers, these are folks who will work in one place for several months before moving to another work assignment elsewhere, often following the seasons—south in winter, north in the summer. As readers of *Nomadland* already know, campgrounds are just one source of employment for these modern-day gypsies, who may pitch in at a beet harvest one month, then work at an Amazon warehouse another. But campgrounds are a mainstay, including those in state and federal parks and forests, not least because part of a work camper's compensation is the free use of an RV site.

At first blush, the match sounds ideal. Work campers already know the campground world, so they can readily relate to customers and answer most if not all their questions. If it's a work camping couple, they frequently complement each other's skills and experience, usually with the woman qualified to work the desk and the man experienced in maintenance or security, so the hiring campground can get two non-duplicative employees for the loss of only one revenue-generating RV site. And because they're living on the campground, unlike local employees who leave the premises each night, they're extra eyes and ears and, in an emergency, an extra set of hands.

Unfortunately, the very qualities that make work campers attractive also can be huge liabilities. Because they've worked at other campgrounds they may have very fixed ideas of how things should be done—and they're not the way you're doing them. If they're a couple and one is unhappy with his or her situation, you risk losing two employees instead of just one. And the RV that brought them to your campground can just as readily whisk them away.

We had one retired couple that worked at Walnut Hills for several years, she as a desk clerk and he, at least 10 years older, on the maintenance staff. Although he did various jobs around the campground, his great joy was to operate one of our zero-turn mowers, but as time went on he had first one accident and then another. Finally, the day he hit a ground-based transformer box hard enough to move it on its concrete pad, I let him know he would no longer be allowed to run the mower. He mulled that over for a day, then told me he was quitting. That didn't come as a surprise—the surprise came when his wife, in a show of solidarity for her mistreated husband, made the same announcement two days later. Just like that we lost a seventh of our workforce a mere ten days before the Fourth of July, one of the three busiest weekends of the year.

It's also possible to read too much into the fact that a work camping couple owns an RV. One of our couple hires arrived in a very large fifth-wheel that we learned only later they had owned just a relatively short while. Whether through inexperience or sheer incompetence, the male half of the couple managed to drop the front end of the unit onto his arm as he was lying under the front axle to adjust a chock. The local fire department responded with its heavy rescue truck and raised the rig enough to pull him out, but then followed two months of medical treatment at the university hospital in Charlottesville. The work camper's arm was saved, but his time was lost to us— and once he was cleared to drive, he and his wife decided they'd had enough of Walnut Hills and they were gone.

Now soured on work camping couples, we gave it one more shot in 2019. Because work campers are planning their assignments at least six months ahead, we agreed that fall to employ a couple for the 2020 season that on paper, at least, looked like outstanding hires. Then the pandemic hit—yet they still showed up in April, as promised, further improving their standing with us. Everything went well for the next four weeks, and we were just starting to feel like we'd made a good decision when our work campers announced they had a family emergency. In Texas. One week before Memorial Day—another of the three busiest weekends of the year—they were gone, pulling up stakes in less than 24 hours without apology and without any more explanation of their circumstances.

We were convinced, without any proof whatsoever, that the "emergency" was simply that a better job offer had come through. Work campers, for obvious reasons, will apply for jobs with several different employers at the same time, accepting the one they find most attractive. But because of the long lead times involved, it's not unusual for new opportunities to crop up and minds to change; the industry is replete with stories of work campers who accept a job and then never show up, or who—as in our case—show up but then disappear at a moment's notice.

(While we eventually decided that couples were more trouble than they're worth, we did have more success with singles—perhaps because they have a harder time getting a placement in the first place. We also created an additional inducement for them to stay through the season by promising a bonus of $1 an hour for every hour they were on the job—provided they were still working for us on Oct. 31—and that seemed to help with attrition.)

There is yet one other labor pool that by definition is more captive, but which over the past couple of years has become harder to tap into: the federal government's J-1 visa program, through which foreign university students can spend their vacations working in the U.S. in seasonal positions. Presented primarily as a cultural exchange opportunity, the J-1 program nevertheless is a mainstay of the American tourist industry, especially in areas like the Wisconsin Dells, whose low year-round population explodes in the summers and the number of needed workers is multiples of the available local workforce.

Quite a few campgrounds, especially labor-intensive ones like the Jellystone franchise or larger campgrounds near national attractions, like the Mount Rushmore KOA, have used J-1 students for years. Unfortunately, we soon learned that because it's more cost-effective for the brokers who match eligible students with employers to place dozens of students at a time rather than just one or two, many were reluctant to take us on. And while we prided ourselves on being in the beautiful and scenic Shenandoah Valley, that didn't have the same cachet with foreign students as Yellowstone or Yosemite national parks, or anything near a major and iconic U.S. city like New York, San Francisco or Washington, D.C. We would not have applicants beating down our doors.

Nonetheless, we did find some brokers who would work

with us (although the first one declined to repeat for a second year) and we did get applicants, although our choices were always quite limited. Our first year we completely lucked out in hiring two German students with excellent English skills who, despite not knowing each other prior to working for us, got along quite well and were personally engaging. But the next year we had only one applicant, from Peru, whose limited grasp of English and extreme shyness led him to avoid talking to us whenever possible, much as we tried to draw him out. Fortunately, we were able to introduce him to a local restaurant owner who'd emigrated from Argentina and needed a part-time dishwasher in the evenings, so our Peruvian student gained both additional income and someone with whom he could chat in Spanish.

Our third go-round with the program was the most difficult. That year we hosted two students from Turkey, so once again we had a pair of foreign workers who could converse in their native tongue—but that, as it turned out, was the only thing they had in common. One, hard-working and eager to improve his English and to learn American ways, came from the Armenian-dominated agricultural east; the other, affecting a world-weary lassitude that found fault with everything and everyone— including his new roommate—was from the metropolitan environs of Istanbul, and a more difficult city mouse-country mouse combination is hard to imagine. By summer's end the country mouse was on the verge of strangling his annoying compatriot, impressing on us the extraordinarily vulnerable position our foreign workers accepted in coming to work for us. If work campers had us at their mercy because of their mobility, the J-1 students were in precisely the opposite situation, isolated thousands of miles from home.

Our spirits lifted in the fourth year, when we hired a fluent English-speaking Russian student and an effusive if less polished Jordanian—and then the pandemic unraveled everything, the J-1 program collapsed everywhere and our new hires became no-shows.

By late 2019, however, our business had rebounded from

our immediate post-KOA slump, and with the savings from our disenfranchisement we had more disposable income than ever. One consequence was that we began raising our starting wage, which at that time was $8.50 an hour, and in the process bumped everyone else up as well. By the end of 2020 every wage earner was making a minimum of $10 an hour, and my hope was to keep pushing that up by at least dollar a year until we hit $15.

The more significant change I felt we finally could afford was to put two of our non-family employees on salary for the first time in 2018, followed by a third the next year, with a commitment to keep them on payroll year-round. This meant that for the first time we actually had a shot at keeping our best employees from one season to the next. Moreover, it meant that while we had no formal sick-leave policy, at least these few employees no longer had to worry about losing income because of illness. None of our employees was getting wealthy working for us, but at least we were moving toward a financially stable environment.

The impact of these changes on our profit and loss statement was notable, as payroll expenses jumped from 26.2% of gross revenues in 2017, our last year as a KOA franchisee— more or less in line with industry norms—to 32.5% of gross in 2019, even though our gross that year was just a hair above what it had been two years earlier. Although the increase nicked our net operating income a tad, almost all of it was covered by our get-out-of-KOA yellow card, and I was certain that we would see increased returns in the years ahead. The future was looking rosy.

"Hey" ride at Walnut Hils.

9. The Disney-fication of camping

ALTHOUGH KOA HAS BEEN A LEADER in the growing commodification of "the outdoor experience," it certainly hasn't been alone. As the RVing phenomenon exploded in recent years, luring hordes of people whose only previous contact with "nature" had been while mowing the lawn, an industry-wide push has sought to convince the public that nature is essentially benign, that she can be encountered on the user's terms, and that there is absolutely no reason why anyone needs to be uncomfortable when doing so.

At one extreme are resorts that permit only motorcoaches, excluding both travel trailers and fifth-wheels (how middle class!), no matter how lavishly decked out, and refusing even to acknowledge the legitimacy of pick-up campers and pop-ups. These are high-end and extraordinarily expensive properties, some even offering sites that include private bathrooms and kitchens under a pavilion adjacent to the RV pad, all set within immaculately groomed and landscaped grounds that include such amenities as clubhouses, heated pools, spas, and tennis and bocci courts. Although technically "campgrounds," in the sense that the people who stay there are transient and providing their own living quarters, such resorts bear as little relationship to camping as does an overnight stay in a Walmart parking lot, the prototypical other extreme.

It's the extremes, however, that tend to define the middle. And as the glitziest RV properties keep pushing the envelope in demonstrating how much "camping" can be just like home, but prettier, the rest of the market falls in behind. The inherently tight quarters of a vehicle that must navigate streets and highways have been expanded through the development of slides. Effective living space also has been increased through multiple powered awnings extending over external kitchens and entertainment centers, accessible via outside compartment doors that enable a camper to share his favorite TV show or mix tape with all his neighbors. Pricier RVs come with dishwashers and washing machines and dryers, heated floors and zoned air conditioning. Heading out for a little communing with nature? No reason why you can't take all the comforts of home with you!

Commercial campgrounds that aren't resorts have stepped up their game as well—and those that don't, quickly get blasted in social media and online reviews for their shortcomings. It wasn't all that long ago that some campgrounds had sites supplied solely by electricity; if you wanted water you could use a communal spigot to fill your tanks, and if you needed to empty your wastewater tanks, there might—or might not—be a dump station. But these days even full hook-up sites are often deemed insufficient if they don't come with internet access robust enough for streaming, and the demand for more electricity to power all those on-board conveniences has grown so great, some campgrounds are questioning whether they'll eventually have to provide 100-amp pedestals— twice today's 50-amp max.

All that is a long way from the earliest days of camping as recreation, when American aristocracy would take to the Adirondacks, hiking through the woods with a supporting cast of porters and cooks to find a likely spot, clear a site and erect heavy canvas tents. The servants did the hard work, of course, but the overall experience was still basically raw: no running water except in a stream, no electricity, pit toilets and a certain vulnerability to cold and wet weather. As related by landscape architect Martin Hogue, such camps—stripped of any but the most vital conveniences—were "literally and figuratively open to the stimuli of natural surroundings."

The supplanting of all that human labor by camping technology can be viewed as a democratization of outdoor access. But it also increasingly insulates those campers from the very experience they claim to be seeking, resulting—again, in Hogue's words—in "the idealization of nature as peaceful and non-threatening." Nature, he added, "is expected to remain comfortable, visually and emotionally inspiring; but its atmospheric effects should be negligible." *

"Atmospheric effects" is a delightful euphemism for nature's discomfiting intrusions into the lives of our campers, who were not bashful about complaining to us about being inconvenienced, or who sometimes would just take matters into their own hands. Few sights I encountered were as chilling as the man I saw one day swinging a long-handled ax toward the mouth of one of our culverts, a gaggle of children clustered excitedly in his wake. "What the hell are you doing?" I yelled as I ran in his direction.

"I'm going after a snake," he yelled back, as if it were the most natural thing in the world.

I managed to get him to back off, brushing aside his contention that he was just protecting the children playing in the

---

*Hogue's relatively rare observations—there's not a lot written about modern-day camping from a sociological or philosophical perspective— can be read in his fascinating essay, "A Short History of the Campsite." Another sample: "The ability to watch a nationally televised baseball game from the concrete pad outside a late-model RV by using campground-provided cable, or to send emails wirelessly from the campsite picnic table—standard amenities at most KOAs—bespeaks the near total elimination of boundaries between home and away. Is this the point at which the labor of camping—or, rather, the absence of it—ceases to hold any of its old, once almost mythical power?"

stream by pointing out that perhaps a less risky response would be to have the children play elsewhere. I didn't rebuke him for the liberties he was taking on someone else's property, or the hazard he was creating for the very children he ostensibly was trying to protect, although I was sorely tempted; and I didn't challenge his conclusion that the snake he'd seen was a water moccasin, even though odds were that it was one of the many non-poisonous water snakes living on the grounds. Any snake our campers saw swimming inevitably got tagged with the water moccasin label (to be fair, there were some of those, too), and if I'd left it to them they'd have slaughtered every snake in sight, just to be on the "safe" side.

But there are lots of other things in nature that, if not a mortal threat, nevertheless can be annoying. Bugs, for example. Campers would freak out over carpenter bees, which we detested because of the damage they inflicted on our many wooden buildings, but they don't sting; they're in-your-face aggressive and they look menacing, but it's one big bluff. Ants were a big deal for some people, who seemed to think they should somehow be guaranteed an RV site without any, and stink bugs were a total gross-out—not least because they often would burrow into an RV and hitch a ride back to a camper's sticks-and-bricks home. Yet no matter how sternly we warned people not to put out their garbage after 11 a.m., when we ran the last pick-up of the day, someone would leave out a bag of trash in the evening for the crows to dissect and other critters to disperse overnight—and, of course, to attract more ants.

Or consider rain. Being outdoors and dealing with rain is as "natural" as one can get, but the slightest chance of precipitation would prompt a smattering of cancellations, even though such forecasts are notoriously unreliable in the mountains. A reservation cancelled less than 48 hours in advance would forfeit the one-night deposit, which often provoked an argument; but the bigger outrage came from campers who were already on site and demanding a refund because they wanted to leave early so they wouldn't get wet. "We don't charge you extra for sunshine, and we don't give you money back for rain," we'd reply.

For some campers, trees were an annoyance: they'd hang too low over the roads, brushing the lustrous paint jobs on their expensive fifth-wheels or motor homes, some of which require a 14-foot clearance. Or they'd block their satellite dishes from picking up a signal. Or they'd drop messy seeds or pods or flowers that would stain their vehicles—or maybe that was the birds? Darkness—otherwise known as night—would be an issue for others, who wanted every square inch of the landscape illuminated. And heaven help us if local farmers spread manure up-wind of the campground, which strictly speaking wasn't an act of nature but which is a natural way to fertilize in an agricultural area, which is where we were.

All this might sound a little silly and meaningless in the bigger scheme of things, except insofar as it attests to a broader neutering of "nature" in which the campground industry is not only complicit, but which it is actively promoting. The buzz about glamping, the relentless paving over and lighting of campsites, the eager accommodation of ever-larger energy-hogging homes on wheels, the steady transformation of campgrounds into amusement parks—all act to increasingly divorce the camping public from the natural world it ostensibly is celebrating. Nature becomes little more than a backdrop for glossy photos of couples sitting beside a campfire, wine glasses in hand, saying to each other, "Wouldn't it be neat if we could have this all the time?"

Meanwhile, as I realized just how sanitized an experience many of our campers wanted, I noted with growing dismay that the actual environment was moving in exactly the opposite direction: the world was going to hell, almost literally. Our search for an ideal campground location had been defined in part by steering clear of identifiable environmental threats, but it was increasingly clear that this had been a fool's errand: there is no escape. Year by year the weather was getting more extreme, from yet another round of all-time temperature highs to record-breaking rainfalls to ever-angrier lightning storms and tornado strikes. And year by year, it started to sink in on me that perhaps the lifestyle and business we had adopted was disproportionally contributing to the problem—that perhaps RVing and camping had become not just oblivious to the natural world, but active contributors toward its demise.

My growing doubt about the viability of this business we'd jumped into came to a head the summer of 2018, when I read a New York Times Magazine edition that devoted an entire issue to a single story, "Losing Earth." This extraordinary journalistic effort focused on the decade of 1979-89, a time of now-inconceivable bipartisan acknowledgment that the science of climate change had been firmly established and that it posed an existential crisis that had to be swiftly addressed, starting with carbon-emission controls. That didn't happen, as climate-change deniers started gaining traction and vested interests pushed back against the disruption of their businesses, and 30 years later the consequences of a loss of bipartisanship—polarized discourse and resulting inaction—are painfully evident.

Over those three decades, more carbon had been released into the atmosphere than in all human history prior to 1989. Stoking the greenhouse effect resulted in higher temperatures worldwide, which heated not just the planet's land surface but its oceans and atmosphere as well, resulting in significantly more airborne moisture. The upshot is that even as some regions are afflicted by profound drought, others get battered by torrential rains and floods. As I wrote in an unpublished essay later that summer, questioning whether an RV lifestyle was sustainable, it seemed as if all of California was in flames, as was much of Colorado. Forest fires closed campgrounds from New Mexico and Arizona north to Yellowstone and into Oregon, Washington, and British Columbia. What wasn't scorched was in danger of drowning, with heavy rains and saturated soils creating epic floods in half-a-dozen states, from Pennsylvania and North Carolina in the east to Tennessee, Iowa, and Montana farther west.

Yet even as Hurricane Florence lumbered ashore that

September, inundating hundreds of square miles of mid-Atlantic coastline and forcing scores of campgrounds to close, the largest RV show on the eastern seaboard was in full swing just a six-hour drive to the north. Sprawling across an area larger than 33 football fields, the annual Hershey RV Show was displaying more than 1,300 recreational vehicles at every possible price point; the West Coast got its turn a month later, when a similarly sized exhibition ran for 10 days in Pomona. The RV industry, in other words, was in full-throated denial that there was anything to worry about. Nothing to see here!

Although matters have only gotten worse[*] since then— could there be anything more ironic than having something called Camp Fire consume Paradise later that same year? — the industry that so ardently promotes the healing properties and aesthetic qualities of the great outdoors has been resolutely silent on its degradation. The industry press, wary of ruffling advertisers' feathers, has no lack of coverage of campgrounds slammed by tornadoes or washed out by floods, but makes absolutely no attempt at explaining why such reports are growing in frequency and severity. Context? We don't need no stinkin' context! It's as if the news were to detail a pattern of shooting deaths and casualties without reporting that there was a war in progress—let the reader figure out why the morgue is filling up.

Even ostensibly independent industry observers for the most part have avoided what they see as a quagmire. When I submitted an essay, titled "Is RVing a sustainable lifestyle? Mother Nature may not think so" to a reader-supported online RV publication, the editor's response was brisk: "I can't get into global

---

[*]How much worse? At this writing, the Dixie Fire in California is already multiples bigger than the Camp Fire and has consumed an area larger than all of Rhode Island. It was being battled, ironically, as the Intergovernmental Panel on Climate Change issued its sixth assessment report, which among a litany of sobering statistics observed that the past decade has in all probability been the hottest the world has experienced in the past 125,000 years, and that atmospheric levels of carbon dioxide have not been this high in at least two million years.

warming. Period. It's hot button stuff. I'd lose 10 percent of my audience, and, frankly, whatever you or I say won't make an ounce of difference and will just open up a political discussion we have told our readers we will leave to others." Except, of course, there are no "others" having that conversation, either.

Meanwhile, the country's only collective voice for campground owners, the National Association of RV Parks and Campgrounds—otherwise known as ARVC—has just as assiduously avoided the subject. Although its annual conventions are stuffed with workshops on reservation systems and how to make a business legally bulletproof against lawsuits, there is not a peep about climate change and environmental degradation, much less any advice on what countermeasures should or could be taken. Why the silence, in the face of an onslaught that threatens the ongoing viability of its membership base? Likely because that's an accurate reflection of the membership's views and political leanings, which skew heavily toward a cliched sense of self-reliant, regulation-hating "independence" that views both government and science with deep suspicion.

That's not to say that ARVC has completely ignored climate change—indeed, as far back as 1998 it adopted a "policy on global climate change." Leading off with a nod to the importance of "the preservation of the Earth's environment and climate," the policy further affirmed that "the preservation of opportunities for Americans to enjoy outdoor recreational opportunities are also of great importance"—but as ARVC made clear, by "preservation" it didn't mean preserving the environment. It meant preserving the regulatory status quo.

Prompting this concern were international negotiations, then underway, over reducing greenhouse emissions. The ARVC policy contended that these reductions would result in higher energy prices and have an adverse effect on the American economy, individual lifestyles and, most critically, opportunities for travel and recreation. Such reductions would be premature because of the "considerable uncertainty surrounding the theories on climate change" and a need for "more research, data collection and scientific analysis." Until the U.S. was able to refine computer models and improve understanding of climate science, the policy concluded, the U.S. Congress should refuse to approve any changes in emissions standards—which, under pressure from numerous similar protests from various vested interests, it did.

More than two decades later, ARVC's position remains unchanged: that the science is uncertain, that more study is needed and that emissions reductions would be bad for the economy in general and the RVing industry in particular. Nor is it open even to raising the subject for membership discussion, as I learned after more than a year of attempting to get the ARVC board of directors to meaningfully revisit the policy. Rebuffed and ignored over many months, I made a final attempt to address the membership directly at ARVC's 2019 convention in Oklahoma City, where I tried to leaflet two separate general sessions and each time was promptly escorted from the ballroom by a tight claque of red-faced ARVC officers. Maybe it was the leaflet headline that got me bounced: "Q: How is ARVC like a brontosaurus? A: Neither knows how to deal with climate change . . . and one is already extinct."

Point made.

Meanwhile, the drumbeat of campgrounds shut down because of smoke from distant forest fires, of travel trailers flipped over by tornadoes, of campground owners shoveling out the mud deposited in their buildings by rampaging flood waters—all that continues with growing frequency, prompting repeated pleas from ARVC for donations to help the afflicted. Clearly, there's a cost to inaction, too; the only question is how much more pain will have to be endured before the industry starts connecting the dots.

Worn to the bone.

10. Whip-sawed by the pandemic

THE ONE THING THAT SAW ME through the many long hours we slaved away at the campground was the annual trip I took each winter. Part of the agreement our family made before buying Walnut Hills, to offset in some small way the abysmal hours we'd be putting in, was that each couple could take a month off between December and February, when business slowed to a crawl. But while this gave Carin and me the opportunity to spend a couple of vacations in warmer weather, she never was keen on traveling. And after she slipped on a pebble—in our driveway! —and broke a hip, any remaining wanderlust was snuffed out of her.

Thus began my solo globe-hopping, to New Zealand and Tasmania, Peru and Patagonia, and usually without incident—until 2020. When I left in mid-February that year, for Japan to visit friends and then to the Himalayas to join a tour group, the pandemic that was about to upend the world economy was barely registering on American consciousness but had already cast a pall over Asia. Flying into famously cloistered Bhutan, our group had to fill out health questionnaires and have our temperatures taken. My acknowledgment that I had picked up a minor cold in Tokyo resulted in more intensive questioning, followed by an admonition that I immediately report any change for the worse; three days later our group leader got a phone call from the kingdom's health administration, asking not only about my health (I was fine) but about that of the four people—asked about by name—who had been seated closest to me on the plane.

So I was astonished, in the early morning hours of March 8, when I deplaned at Dulles International Airport and was waved through customs without a pause. No one looked at my luggage, no one asked me where I had been or inquired about any medical complaints I might have. I was lucky. Less than a week later all inbound flights into the U.S. were routed through just 13 airports nationwide, resulting in waits of up to seven hours for passengers jammed by the thousands into endless queues that served as Covid 19 petri dishes. And three weeks after that, the roof caved in.

On March 30, Virginia Governor Ralph Northam issued a "temporary stay at home" edict that contained a single sentence upending our lives, calling for a "cessation of all reservations for overnight stays of less than 14 nights at all privately-owned camp-grounds." Inexplicably, the order did not extend to any other sector of the transient hospitality industry, such as hotels, motels, resorts and B&Bs. Maddeningly, "temporary" in this case was to run until June 10, the longest stay-at-home order in the United States and extending well into camping season. And, just like that, we were teetering on the edge of insolvency.

Since 90% of our business consisted of short-term camp-ers, and because a lot of our repeat campers made reservations a year or more in advance, we had tens of thousands of dollars in bookings that had to be moved or cancelled. The first week of April was spent burning up the phone lines, calling literally scores of campers about the situation and asking them to reschedule. Many did, but we still had to void more than $20,000 in reservation fees—and that was just for reservations made for that month. Moreover, that came on top of cancellations that had already been made in March, before the shut-down order, as our more cautious campers changed their plans without any official prodding.

Looking for any possible way to keep cash flowing, we started booking long-term stays on sites that had been exclusively short-term—at a rate roughly one-third the overnight price. Moreover, to encourage bookings within the letter of the governor's proclamation, we also offered two-week stays for the price of one. Both moves meant we were offering huge discounts on even our most favored sites, but some money was better than none and we had no clue how long this state of affairs would continue.

At the same time, we realized that the governor's order was going to create a huge problem for the RVing public traveling in and through Virginia. America's highways were being crisscrossed by emergency workers and medical personnel rushing from one pandemic crisis point to the next. Snowbirds who had gone south for the winter were trying to get back home in the north. Full-timers everywhere were desperately looking for a place to land after they got kicked out by campgrounds that were completely shutting down.* With Interstate 81 traversing 325 miles of mountainous Virginia landscape, where were these people going to stop, even if only for a night?

Once again deciding to follow just the letter of Gov. Northam's edict, we stopped taking overnight reservations—but let the RVing public know that the long pull-throughs at the front of the campground were theirs for the taking, no charge. Want to make a donation? Swell—but don't feel obliged. The

---

*Campendium, an RV camping app, calculated that spring that 44% of all RV sites in the country had been shut down by federal, state and county officials, evicting untold numbers of RVers in the process. Meanwhile, there are as many as one million full-timers in the U.S., although reliable numbers are non-existent.

emailed response was overwhelmingly supportive and most nights a handful of travelers would take us up on our offer, some staying for free and some kicking in as much as $50 for the night, but almost all leaving notes of heartfelt gratitude and thanks.

During all this scrambling, however, I kept getting hung up on the sheer incongruity of what was happening. Of all the possible housing options for travelers, none can match the isolating potential of an RV. Anyone traveling in a motor coach, travel trailer or fifth-wheel has his or her own little bubble, with their own kitchen and cookware, their own bathroom, and their own linens. Aside from pumping gas or buying groceries, no one in an RV has to interact with anyone else—and gas pumps are outdoors and socially distanced already, while everyone in a pandemic has to get groceries, regardless of where they live. Why on earth would the governor single out campgrounds for a ban on short-term stays while exempting the rest of the lodging industry?

I never did get a direct answer, despite a couple of letters to the governor that he ignored. But word quickly filtered through the state's campground association that a state politician had been told by a friend that there were people partying at a campground on Virginia's Eastern Shore, the implication being that RV campgrounds were sybaritic incubators of disease. The claim was never verified, but this game of telephone proceeded up the ranks of state government until it reached the ears of Gov. Northam, who apparently took it at face value and slammed the gates shut. The state politician who got the ball rolling, meanwhile, went on to justify his hysterics by lamenting that "travelers to the campgrounds will take all our food."

But then, on May 8, the pendulum swung the other way: Gov. Northam announced he would lift his short-term camping ban the following week, several weeks ahead of schedule. The timing was fortuitous, because we were just about to start cancelling all Memorial Day weekend reservations. But the announcement also opened the floodgates, as a public suffering from weeks of cabin fever overwhelmed our phone lines and on-line reservation system in a desperate attempt to book sites. Flipping from drought to monsoon, we now had to figure out how to shoehorn campers into a patchwork of a reservation grid that was broken up by monthly campers staying in overnight sites, as well as two-week blocs made inaccessible by our "buy one, get two" deal.

There were other constraints that had to be explained to the callers as well. Masking was required. Social distancing rules remained in place, and facilities that "encourage gathering" could not be reopened. That meant our game room and enclosed pavilion would have to remain shut—as would the swimming pool. Indeed, those amenities ended up being closed all year long, reopening only the next May. There also wouldn't be any organized activities for the kids, and no weekend concerts.

But the biggest—unspoken—constraint on what we could or couldn't offer was our inability to staff up sufficiently. We simply didn't have enough bodies to do all the work that this epic resurgence of demand was creating. Heading into the previous winter we had tried to retain as many employees as possible, even when there wasn't enough work to justify the expense, and so entered the new year with a payroll of eight. By early May, despite every recruiting approach we could devise—including turning to a local temp agency—we were able to increase that to only nine, and two of the nine were the work campers who would jump ship a couple of weeks later.

The best we could do for most of the season thereafter was to have a staff of ten, or about two-thirds of what we needed. Initially, as registrations in March declined 29%, then plummeted 89% in April, that wasn't a problem. Registration still declined in May, by a more modest 23%, but as the tsunami rolled over us thereafter, camper demand was so strong that we finished the year a hair above our record-setting number of registrations in 2019. That meant roughly 50% more than the usual number of people crowded in for the balance of the season, which was a better problem than the alternative but one that just about killed us, given our thin staffing.

Meanwhile, in addition to the increased workload, we had to contend with significant pushback from campers resisting the social distancing and masking requirements that were being mandated both by the state and by us. Because we took the risk of infection very seriously, we had installed a Plexiglas shield in front of the entire registration counter as early as March, stockpiled free face masks and disinfectant wipes for our staff and customers, and posted a sign on the office door announcing MUST WEAR MASK in apocalypse-sized type. We also announced on our web site and Facebook page that anyone entering our registration office would be required to wear a mask; if that was not possible, for any reason, we would help them outside.

And yet there still were people who would argue. Time and again, we would have arriving campers stroll in who acted shocked—shocked! —when told they would have to don a mask. Most readily relented, but on at least a couple of occasions we had people turn on their heels and announce that they were taking their business elsewhere. Where that might have been wasn't clear, since the entire state was under the same mandate, but the brow-beating approach favored by some campers determined to get their way presumably led them to think they would prevail somewhere else. And they may have been right.

To be fair, most of our campers were only too happy to go along with our strict policies, and indeed, quite a few let us know they had specifically selected Walnut Hills because of what we posted on our web site and on social media about the protocols we were demanding. And, tellingly, the U.S. Travel Association reported in mid-June that 61% of American travelers cited "poor 'pandemic etiquette' behavior by others" as being a significant factor in their travel planning.

But adding to the poor pandemic etiquette, and therefore to our overall stress levels, was a parallel decline in broader campground etiquette. The wave of customers now inundating our campground was not just the traditional camping public in more concentrated numbers, but also a groundswell of first-timers lured by the same observations that had me questioning Gov. Northam's initial shut-down order: what could be a safer way to vacation at a time of social-distancing and cocooning? Campers would repeatedly tell us they had just bought an RV or were borrowing one for the first time from friends or family so they could check out this exciting "new" way to vacation. Rental RVs became an increasingly common—and disconcerting—sight, and RVshare, a peer-to-peer RV rental company, reported a 650% increase in business in mid-May compared to the previous year. Publications of every description, from local dailies to the Wall Street Journal, further fanned the flames by reporting on the allure of traveling in a self-contained bubble at a time of historically low gas prices.

In addition to coping—sometimes badly—with all the challenges faced by any first-time RV operators, such as learning how to back into a site or how to hook up their utilities,[*] many of the new arrivals demonstrated a lack of prior exposure to campground "culture" and, in too many cases, no apparent desire to learn it. Letting dogs run off-leash, cutting across other sites, ignoring quiet hours, using fire pits as trash heaps—these and a score of other offenses proliferated like never before, leading to more camper complaints to us and in turn placing more demands on a staff already stretched too thin.[**]

As the summer wore on, we began to wear down. By early

---

[*]High on the list of transgressions: the willingness of some new campers to stick a sewer hose into any pipe in the ground without first determining if it was indeed a sewer connection—and not, say, a water cut-off valve. A few years earlier we had capped every sewer connection with a yellow spring- closing cap, but even our admonitions to use only those color-coded pipes for dumping sewage sometimes went unheeded, much to the maintenance crew's dismay.

[**]Even a year later the problem persisted. As reported in the June 2021 issue of Woodall's Campground Magazine, campground owners continued to see "a significant increase in unruly guests with little or no knowledge of campground etiquette." The article quoted a Foxboro, Mass. campground operator saying that many of her new campers were "hotel guests" with a sense of entitlement. "They are anxious to get out and be campers, but they're not campers," she complained.

fall, as I looked at our staff in general and at our family members in particular, I realized that the spark was gone. We were all going through the motions, but with a certain resignation, and the backlog of abandoned or neglected maintenance jobs kept growing. Our people were notably tired, dragging in to work later and later or calling out sick altogether, with migraines or other ailments. With both Erika and Mitch showing that their hearts were no longer in their jobs, and with me pushing 73 and less willing to absorb the punishment of picking up everyone else's slack, I tentatively suggested to Carin that maybe it was time to think about selling.

You'd have thought I'd presented her with a diamond necklace.

*   *   *

Although we were nearing the end of only the third year of our second five-year plan, selling a campground historically took up to two years, so I wasn't too concerned that I'd be breaking faith with our kids if I broached the idea of a sale. But I was more worried about Carin's reaction: after all, owning Walnut Hills and operating it successfully for eight years, despite our many challenges, had been the culmination of that fireside dream first articulated so many decades earlier. And despite all the hard work and high stress—or perhaps because of that—we had a degree of financial independence and autonomy neither of us had known before.

Yet when I raised the issue with Carin, she responded with enormous relief and enthusiasm. Living in the vinyl palace, with its annual mouse invasion and unstoppable dust infiltration and the nearby rumbling of diesel engines at all hours of the day and night, apparently had lost its charm. Sidelined by her broken hip and own advancing age, she had had progressively less involvement with the campground even as my involvement grew because of the increased business and our inadequate staffing. Rather than bringing us together, Walnut Hills was driving us apart—a not uncommon dynamic among family-owned campgrounds, as I had observed over the years. So yes, she said. Absolutely. Sell the damn place.

I told Mitch and Erika about our decision in late October, as our season was winding down, explaining that the protracted process of seeking a buyer would be a good opportunity for them to be thinking about next steps in their lives. Some of the sweat equity we'd be extracting from the business would be going to them, I said—a nest-egg for further schooling, or specialized job training, or a down payment on a house. To my surprise, and despite being obviously beaten down by the job, Mitch said he'd hang in there and seek to continue in his position under new ownership. Erika, on the other hand, noticeably brightened at the possibilities. And neither tried to argue against the move, confirming for me that it was indeed the right step for us to take.

The first week in November, I contacted a broker who had been chasing our business for at least the previous two years, asking him for a description of his fees and services. He responded with a lengthy questionnaire, based on which he would provide me with a preliminary estimate of how he thought the campground should be priced and what he would want in compensation: I had almost finished filling it out when I got a generic email asking if I was thinking about selling my campground. What the heck, I thought. It wouldn't hurt to respond.

"We're in the early stages of preparing paperwork for a broker, so yes, we're interested," I replied. "On the other hand, I suspect we may be too small (43 acres, 150 sites with cabins, $800,000 in gross revenues) or too tilted toward non-seasonals to be of interest to you. If I'm wrong, give me a call or email with a response."

Turned out we were *exactly* what Land Lease America was after.

Taking wing.

11. Throwing in the towel

A LITTLE MORE THAN EIGHT years after taking possession of the Staunton/Walnut Hills KOA, we sold the Walnut Hills Campground and RV Park to a pair of young, smart and ambitious guys who have been rolling up similar properties as quickly as they can. We were only the fourth owners in the campground's 52-year history, so as I wrote at the time, our relatively short tenure might create the impression that we lacked stick-to-it-iveness. But as I also observed, campground owners these days are like dogs, at least in a temporal sense: each year spent catering to an increasingly demanding RV crowd is equivalent to eight or nine years of a normal human's. No wonder that the average tenure for campground owners is only seven years.

Everything is moving more quickly these days. Following that initial cold-call email from Land Lease America in mid-November and my cautious response, a quick reply from one of the principals led to a rapid-fire exchange of more emails, descriptions, financial statements and checking of references. I emailed the broker whose questionnaire I had been filling out to thank him for his response but to alert him to the possibility that I might already have a buyer. The two-year window I had been contemplating for finding a buyer and concluding a sale was suddenly, inexplicably being compressed into a fraction of that time.

Or perhaps not inexplicably, after all. Because as I looked around, I realized that we were all in play—some more than others. The poster child for valuation excess was our nearest campground neighbor, Shenandoah Acres, which was sold in 2020 to a holding company for $3 million—which then turned around and sold it less than a year later to Sun RV Resorts for $17 million. But other campgrounds throughout Virginia, many owned by the same families for much longer than we owned Walnut Hills, also got gobbled up within the space of a few months: Misty Mountain, Small Country, Gloucester Point Jellystone.

Land Lease America, the company to whose email I responded, owned only three campgrounds at the time that we started our negotiations but managed a handful of others, all KOAs, across the country. By December they had bought a fourth campground, in Michigan, and were looking to acquire as many as ten in 2021 alone. Given how many balls they had in the air, I probably should not have been surprised at how quickly our talks bogged down: a flying start in which we reached rapid agreement on the broad strokes began to stumble in January on the fine points. When it became clear that an anticipated early April closing was starting to slip into May, I had the purchase agreement amended to stipulate that if we didn't close by May 17, closing would be delayed by at least two weeks so we could claim the income for Memorial Day weekend. That, apparently, broke the logjam. May 17 it was.

The events of the following few months were predictable, sometimes sadly so but undoubtedly in keeping with the new realities. An outside manager, who had been a full-time RVer for a couple of years and had most recently been operating a marina, moved into the vinyl palace and quickly started making changes that he thought reasonable. Erika was offered a clerk's position, which amounted to a demotion and confirmed for her that it made more sense to move on with her life elsewhere. Mitch declared that he wanted to stay in the double-wide that he'd worked so hard on rehabilitating, and so even though he'd agreed with me a few months earlier that his heart was no longer in the job, continued as "lead" maintenance worker—there no longer was a "head of" title for the slot, in a company that prides itself on having a flattened organizational chart.

New ownership proved no more capable than us of solving the staffing problems we'd faced, so despite a short-lived uptick in the ranks of the maintenance staff—due mainly to several former employees who'd been fired or had quit but saw an opportunity under new ownership, only to have history repeat itself—the campground continued to operate short-handed. Some relief was provided by a decision to stop splitting firewood—a job that had fallen almost entirely to me in the last year—and instead to buy it, already packaged, from an outside vendor.

The overwhelmed front desk clerks, meanwhile, were instructed not to answer the phone if they had a customer in front of them— reversing our policy that all calls had to be answered within three rings and either put on hold or a message taken for a call back—allowing those calls to roll over into voice mail. Or to get lost. Increasingly, campers were encouraged to bypass the phone altogether and book directly online, which from the campground's point of view allowed for a more efficient use of manpower.

Rates, inevitably, started going up—as they probably would have had we continued to own the campground, although not by as much. The biggest change in this regard was a move to dynamic pricing, which we had resolutely refused to implement but which is gradually becoming standard across the industry, as it already is in hotels and airlines. That means no rate sheets, and no straightforward answer to the question, "What does it cost to stay at your campground?" as rates fluctuate within a certain range depending on supply and demand. The range itself may change at any time, and the cost of a site will move up within that range as demand increases and decline if demand drops off. That's very efficient, too—at least, again, from the campground's perspective.

Other efficiencies included going to a biweekly pay period, with paychecks written and mailed from LLA's centralized bookkeeping office, instead of the weekly paychecks we wrote and distributed each Sunday for the workweek that had ended the previous day. A battery of security cameras was set up in the registration area and around the building, allowing monitoring of campers and employees alike. The hours for delivery of firewood were shortened, and a later closing on the weekends was not instituted. In various ways, in other words, work was outsourced, centralized or eliminated. Whether that will fulfill the new owners' vow to become "the most hospitable company in the world" remains to be seen.

*   *   *

A month after moving into our newly purchased home in Staunton, just half a mile from Erika and our two grandsons, Carin and I sat on our back deck in the shade of a huge maple tree as the setting sun gradually let the air cool. The house had been owned by the same couple for 35 years, and it was they who had planted the maple, as well as the peach, pear, apple, and fig trees on the third of an acre that we now owned. We were drinking Argentinian Malbec from long-stemmed glasses, admiring the fireflies flitting in and around the flowering bushes beneath the deck.

"You know," I said to her, "it's paradoxical to me that we had to move from a campground surrounded by forest and farms to the middle of a city for some peace and quiet. It's quieter here than it ever was at the vinyl palace. "

"Less dusty, too," she answered, raising her glass in salutation.

Afterword

THE TALE I'VE RELATED, while all true, is in a sense myopic: to the extent that it is a story of a particular campground over a particular time span, it lacks broader context. Stepping back from the subject can alter one's perceptions, and in the process create a more nuanced view.

The bigger picture may be reflected in the campground and RV park industry's claims of approximately $6.5 billion in revenue each year (roughly 8,000 times Walnut Hills' annual gross), split between 12,200 campgrounds on public land and 13,900 commercial campgrounds like Walnut Hills. That, in turn, would be only a small slice of the $114 billion that the RV Industry Association—which represents RV builders and suppliers—claims its products and ancillary services contribute annually to the American economy, including $25.6 billion lumped into an "RV campgrounds and travel" category.

Yet despite these claims and estimates, one thing abundantly clear is that no one has a good handle on the commercial campground sector. Two separate studies commissioned in recent years by the National Park Service, which is trying to figure out how to improve its own campground facilities, observed that the private sector is too fragmented and underreported to come to any broad conclusions. Virtually all campground industry research focuses on "what equipment people were purchasing rather than where, how or why people were camping," asserted a 2019 report for the NPS prepared by consulting firm CBRE.

Similarly, a 2020 analysis by CHM Government Services lamented that "there is no equivalent of Smith Travel Research, a data aggregator for the lodging industry, for the private sector campground industry." So, for example, while CHM could report that the National Park Service had 8,585 RV pads—most of which do not have utility hook-ups—no one really knows how many RV or tent sites are provided by the commercial sector.

All this is important for a couple of reasons. First, it means that much of the information about private campgrounds that is generated on a regular basis by KOA and ARVC, among others, must be regarded skeptically. ARVC, for example, has roughly 3,100 members, which suggests that it represents less than a quarter of all commercial campgrounds—and even that is an over-estimate because its includes some public facilities. Meanwhile, ARVC's 2020 "Industry Trends and Insights Report," the all-encompassing title notwithstanding, was based on answers from only 479 self-selected respondents—15% of ARVC's total membership, and less than 4% of the commercial campground universe. Its "trends" and "insights" therefore are expressed in percentages that have dubious value, such as the assertion that 45% of respondent campgrounds had increased expenses due to the Covid-19 pandemic.

In short, it's impossible to characterize the "average" or "typical" campground.

The other significance of these numbers is the extent to which they underscore the fragmentation of the commercial sector. Much has been made, in recent years (and to some extent in this book), of the consolidation and corporatization of the commercial sector—and such a trend is indeed underway. But it is still in its infancy. The three largest owners of U.S. campgrounds—Equity Lifestyle Properties, Sun Communities and KOA—collectively generate less than 10% of all industry revenue. Equity Lifestyle Properties owns a bit more than 206 campgrounds under the Thousand Trails and Encore RV Resorts labels; Sun Communities owns an additional 150-plus, including 13 Jellystone franchises.

Meanwhile, although KOA claims more than 500 campgrounds in its franchise network, it owns only 30 or so outright. Under the KOA umbrella, on the other hand, are several private groups that own multiple KOAs and continue to acquire more, including Recreational Adventures Co., which owns 14, and the Bell family out of San Diego, owner of seven. Land Lease America and its subsidiary, LLA Hospitality, which bought Walnut Hills, may have surpassed that many KOAs as of this writing.

All of which is to say that several major players are indeed emerging, with many more campgrounds due to get rolled up in various portfolios—but there are many, many more commercial campgrounds that remain independent, ranging from the very smallest to the very largest. Indeed, the three biggest campgrounds in the U.S. are all family owned, built up over multiple generations in Myrtle Beach, S.C.

The other myopic aspect of the story I've told is that it suffers from the limitations of any first-hand account: it focuses on the events that come most readily to mind, not necessarily those that are most typical or representative. It is, in other words, in some sense sensationalistic: true, but with distorted emphasis.

I write this because friends and family members to whom I entrusted the original manuscript for this book all commented on its overall negative tone. As one wrote: "Your account dwells on the challenges, and fails to mention much of the good times, the lucky breaks, the rewarding accomplishments. If you are going to tell 'dreamers' that there is still room for them, perhaps you should also let them in on what you've found of value in the experience. If it's not there, you should be telling them instead to run for the hills!"

Guilty as charged. There *were* good times, touching encounters and quietly satisfying accomplishments over those eight-plus years—we could not have lasted that long without them. For all of the hard work involved, we took great satisfaction in the many improvements we were able to make, from planting several dozen trees throughout the campground to building the dog park to upgrading the playground. We had campers and employees who presented us with unexpected small gifts, such as the rock painted by a young girl of me driving our "terrainables," a string of six barrel cars that I would hook up to a golf car and haul around the campground giving rides to little (and sometimes not-so-little) campers. Or the photographs of the campground taken by another of our campers, framed and hung in an office display. Or the bird bath and specially ordered signs bestowed on us by Penny, our very first gardener.

Moreover, while I've detailed the problems we had with staffing, I neglected to acknowledge the many outstanding employees who helped us keep it all together. There's Penny, of course, and her partner, Linda, who was a stalwart presence on the front desk. Tammy, our most excellent housekeeper. Angela, who kept returning year after year even though we had to lay her off every winter. James, on the maintenance crew, who worked too slowly but only because he paid exquisite care to what he was doing, and so made his time worthwhile.

In writing as I have, I did not mean to slight these and many other people, nor to ignore the many uplifting things that were done on our behalf. Rather, I wanted to highlight the more problematic aspects of an industry that is determined not to acknowledge them, and which is more committed to portraying only its sunnier aspects, *a la* Disneyland (or, more darkly, Westworld). Anyone who wants to find out how wonderful it is to camp or to own a campground has no shortage of reading material. This book is, in effect (and with apologies to Paul Harvey), the rest of the story.

So yes, there is still room for the dreamers who, sitting beside a campfire, muse about how neat it would be to actually own a piece of dirt to rent out to RVers and tenters. Just be careful what you wish for!